PROCLAMATION:
Aids for Interpreting the Lessons of the Church Year

EASTER

SERIES C

Howard G. Hageman
and
J. C. Beker

FORTRESS PRESS   Philadelphia, Pennsylvania

COPYRIGHT © 1974 BY FORTRESS PRESS

All rights reserved. No part of this publication may be reproduced, stored in a retrieval system, or transmitted in any form or by any means, electronic, mechanical, photocopying, recording, or otherwise, without the prior permission of the copyright owner.

Library of Congress Catalog Card Number 73-88346

ISBN 0-8006-4052-7

Second printing 1974

4458E74   Printed in U.S.A.   1-4055

General Preface

Proclamation: Aids for Interpreting the Lessons of the Church Year is a series of twenty-five books designed to help clergymen carry out their preaching ministry. It offers exegetical interpretations of the lessons for each Sunday and many of the festivals of the church year, plus homiletical ideas and insights.

The basic thrust of the series is ecumenical. In recent years the Episcopal church, the Roman Catholic church, the United Church of Christ, and the Lutheran and Presbyterian churches have adopted lectionaries that are based on a common three-year system of lessons for the Sundays and festivals of the church year. *Proclamation* grows out of this development, and authors have been chosen from all of these traditions. Some of the contributors are parish pastors; others are teachers, both of biblical interpretation and of homiletics. Ecumenical interchange has been encouraged by putting two persons from different traditions to work on a single volume, one with the primary responsibility for exegesis and the other for homiletical interpretation.

Despite the high percentage of agreement between the traditions, both in the festivals that are celebrated and the lessons that are appointed to be read on a given day, there are still areas of divergence. Frequently the authors of individual volumes have tried to take into account the various textual traditions, but in some cases this has proved to be impossible; in such cases we have felt constrained to limit the material to the Lutheran readings.

The preacher who is looking for "canned sermons" in these books will be disappointed. These books are one step removed from the pulpit: they explain what the lessons are saying and suggest ways of relating this biblical message to the contemporary situation. As such they are springboards for creative thought as well as for faithful proclamation of the word.

The two authors of this volume of *Proclamation* are Howard G. Hageman, President of New Brunswick Theological Seminary, New Brunswick, N. J., and Johan Christiaan Beker, Professor of New Testament, Princeton Theological Seminary, Princeton, N. J. Dr. Hageman, who serves as editor and homiletician of this volume, was for twenty-eight years pastor of North Reformed Church, Newark, N. J. He began his ministry at that church when he graduated from seminary in 1945 and left it only when he was called back to that same seminary in 1973 to serve as president. Preaching has been one of the particular focuses of Dr. Hageman's ministry, and he has published a number of books in this area as well as some guides for Bible study. He is a regular columnist for *The Church Herald*, the magazine of the Reformed Church in America, and a member of the editorial board of *Theology Today*. Dr. Beker, who has provided the exegesis for the present volume, is, like Dr. Hageman, of Dutch extraction. He received his basic education and theological training in Holland and came to the United States to do graduate work in theology. Since he was awarded the Ph.D. by the University of Chicago in 1955, he has taught New Testament at Union Theological Seminary, Pacific School of Religion, and Princeton Theological Seminary. He has written numerous journal and encyclopedia articles; most recently he was coauthor of a book entitled *Commitment Without Ideology* (Philadelphia: United Church Press, 1973). Since 1951 he has been a lay member of the Protestant Episcopal Church.

Table of Contents

General Preface	iii
The Resurrection of Our Lord, Easter Day	1
Easter Evening *or* Easter Monday	8
The Second Sunday of Easter	14
The Third Sunday of Easter	21
The Fourth Sunday of Easter	27
The Fifth Sunday of Easter	34
The Sixth Sunday of Easter	40
The Ascension of Our Lord	46
The Seventh Sunday of Easter	52

The Resurrection of Our Lord
Easter Day

Lutheran	Roman Catholic	Episcopal	Presbyterian and UCC
Exod. 15:1–11	Acts 10:34a, 37–43	Isa. 25:6–9	Exod. 15:1–11
1 Cor. 15:1–11	Col. 3:1–4	Col. 3:1–4	1 Cor. 15:20–26
Luke 24:1–11	John 20:1–9	Luke 24:1–10	Luke 24:13–35

EXEGESIS

First Lesson: Exod. 15:1-11. The victory song in Exod. 15:1–12 is an expansion into three stanzas of the well-known song in Exod. 15:21 which is sung by Miriam, the sister of Moses and Aaron, to celebrate the exodus of the people of Israel out of Egypt under the leadership of Moses and their escape from the pursuing Egyptian army. The exodus marks the birthday of Israel as a nation for it made possible Israel's pilgrimage to the promised land.

The victory song celebrates the miraculous crossing of the Sea of Reeds and attributes the miracle of Israel's salvation to the direct saving intervention of God. "Thy right hand, O Lord, glorious in power; thy right hand, O Lord, shatters the enemy" (v. 6). "Thou didst stretch out thy right hand, the earth swallowed them" (v. 12). In retrospect the Christian church understood itself as the new Israel and has always seen the exodus through the Red Sea as a typology for its own birthday—the day of the resurrection, when Christ was raised from the dead "by the power of God" (cf. 1 Cor. 6:14).

Thus in 1 Corinthians 10 Paul appropriates the exodus for the Christian community and assimilates the destiny of the old Israel to that of the new Israel: "I want you to know, brethren, that our fathers were all under the cloud, and all passed through the sea, and all were baptized into Moses in the cloud and in the sea. . . . they drank from the supernatural Rock which followed them, and the Rock was Christ. . . . Now these things are warnings for us. . . ."

The exodus became the interpretative means to explicate the meaning of the death and resurrection of Christ. Paul used this means especially in Romans 6 where he portrays the new resurrection life of the Christian as a pilgrimage out of baptism into Christ in "newness of life" toward the promised land, the coming kingdom of God.

Thus the meaning of baptism circles around the understanding of the death and resurrection of Christ. The Christian is baptized into Christ's death but is also raised with Christ into newness of life. And as the exodus followed the captivity in Egypt, so the resurrection follows our captivity to death. It is remarkable that in Rom. 6:4 Paul uses a term that is similar to one in Exodus 15 which attributes the validation of the promise to the right hand and glory of God: "so that as Christ was raised from the dead by the *glory* of the Father, we too might walk in newness of life."

Just as the passage through the Red Sea enables Israel to walk toward the promised land, so Christ's passage through death, and our baptism into his death, enables us to walk toward the coming kingdom of God.

Second Lesson: 1 Cor. 15:1–11. 1 Corinthians 15 is undoubtedly the most crucial chapter about the resurrection in the NT. It gives us not only the earliest account of the resurrection, but also the only account by an apostolic witness. All the other resurrection accounts in the synoptic Gospels and in John are by later writers and contain a good deal of legendary material.

The resurrection account here comes in the context of the Corinthians' misunderstanding of the resurrection. Karl Barth has suggested that this chapter on the resurrection forms the climax of Paul's letter to the Corinthians: all their difficulties and divisions as reported in the earlier chapters stem finally from a basic misunderstanding of the resurrection. It is not the case that the Corinthians disbelieve the resurrection of Christ as v. 12 might suggest. They believe in the resurrection of Christ but interpret it in such a spiritualistic fashion that they deny any relation of the body with the spiritual resurrection. They consider themselves already spiritually raised with Christ in terms of their inner selves. Thus they hold to a belief which the pastoral Epistles attribute to Hymenaeus and Philetus "who have swerved from the truth by holding that the resurrection is past already" (2 Tim. 2:18). This belief leads to a spiritual egoism and feeling of perfection which are prevalent in all the actions of the Corinthians: they are no longer concerned with their moral and "bodily" obligations on earth and with the well-being of their brethren. A future resurrection of the body is what the Corinthians reject. Hence their disinterest in all their "worldly" actions.

Paul insists on the ecumenical nature of the resurrection witness: "Whether then it was I or they, so we preach and so you believed" (v. 11). Over against the erroneous resurrection faith of the Corinthians, Paul comes to speak about the unanimous apostolic resurrection faith. He insists that this resurrection faith is the common tradition of the Christian church. With a rabbinic formula he stresses that he has only "handed over" to the Corinthians what he himself has "received" from the primitive Jerusalem church. Thereupon he recites a traditional creedal formula which runs from v. 3b through v. 5. He adds more testimony and ends it with Christ's personal appearance to himself. Words of self-humiliation are coupled with words of pride. Although an "abortive child" and unworthy to be called an apostle because of his earlier persecution of the church, he states that Christ nevertheless appeared to him and fitted him out for his apostolic task. "His grace toward me was not in vain. . . . I worked harder than any of them."

Keep in mind that an apostle is someone who is a missionary through a personal appearance of the risen Christ; Paul claims to be the least but also the last apostle and he equates the appearance of Christ to Peter and the Twelve with Christ's appearance to him.

Gospel: Luke 24:1-11. Luke 24:1–11 should actually not be read in isolation from the rest of the chapter. This chapter contains three basic sections: vv. 1–11, the message of the angels to the women; vv. 13–35, the appearance of Christ to the two disciples on the Emmaus road; vv. 36–53, Christ's appearance to the disciples and his subsequent (probable) ascension.

The two basic elements in Luke's resurrection story, as in the resurrection stories in Matthew and John, are: (1) the tradition of the empty tomb, with (Matthew, Luke, John) or without (Mark) appearances to women (Matthew, Luke) or to women and disciples (John); (2) the tradition of the personal appearance of Christ to the disciples. Within the tradition we see a clear sequence: gradually the two elements are woven together. At first (Mark) we have only an announcement to the women at the empty tomb; the disciples are not connected with the empty tomb. Subsequently, appearances of Christ, which were first separate from the tomb, are connected with it as in Matthew, where Christ appears himself after the angel to the women. Later on the disciples become connected with the empty tomb, so that in John we have a double connection: in John not only are the two main disciples connected with the empty tomb, but Christ also appears to Mary Magdalene there.

In Luke 24 this connection is not yet completed: there is no appearance of Christ to the women and the disciples are not clearly connected with the empty tomb. Although some manuscripts add a v. 13, with the report of Peter's visit to the tomb, this and subsequent visits do nothing to lift the doubt about the resurrection of Christ. It is important to observe that in Luke, apostolic witness to the resurrection is not moderated by the empty tomb, which does not dispel doubt, but by Christ's personal appearance to Peter and to the Emmaus disciples (Luke 24:34, 35). Luke 24:1–11 indicates the belief of the women over against the unbelief of the disciples: "These words seemed to them an idle tale and they did not believe them" (v. 11). Yet the women here are witnesses to the resurrection faith: they are to remember the passion and resurrection predictions of Jesus which he made while he was still in Galilee.

Keep in mind that Luke locates the resurrection not in Galilee as do Mark, Matthew, and John 21, but in Jerusalem and there only. But notice how beautifully Luke illustrates in chap. 24 the slow overcoming of doubt by faith.

HOMILETICAL INTERPRETATION

Almost from its beginning, the Christian community saw the closest parallel between the deliverance of Israel from Egypt and its own deliverance by the death and rising again of its Lord. In both events the essential theme was the same—*victory;* but in neither case was the victory the result of human skill or striving. It was an unmerited act of the grace and goodness of God.

It is for this reason that the song of Moses can also serve as an Easter hymn. The new Israel of the Christian community has in Easter experienced the same mighty act of God which the old Israel experienced in the crossing of the Red Sea. This may at first seem difficult for us to understand because the common interpretation of Easter in our time is that of a festival of private immortality in which all of the battle metaphors of the song of Moses seem inappropriate.

But private immortality, though certainly not unrelated to the Easter gospel, is just as certainly not its major thrust. Easter is the unexpected victory after the fierce battle of Calvary. All the forces of evil and death hurled themselves against the cross to destroy Jesus Christ. And at the close of Good Friday it seemed as though they had been successful.

Then came the mighty and unexpected act of God in the resurrection on Easter morning, a reversal even more stunning than that which occurred when the children of Israel crossed over in safety. The identification of the two events was inevitable. "I will sing to the Lord, for he has triumphed gloriously. . . . The Lord is my strength and my song, and he has become my salvation."

Some wiseacre has remarked that in Western Christendom we have worshiped a crucified Christ who is risen, whereas early Christianity worshiped a risen Christ who was crucified. Certainly both medieval art and Reformation dogma have put a heavy emphasis on the crucifixion, the one by the huge and often gruesomely realistic crucifixes which dominated the entire church building, the other by its heavy emphasis on sin and forgiveness through the atoning death of Christ. In either case, the Easter gospel has tended to be something of an appendix.

Though no one wants to eliminate the significance of that atoning death, it is also true that Easter is the last word and that the Christ who confronts us today is risen and alive. That is why Paul makes such a point of the resurrection of Christ as the keystone of his gospel, carefully lining up the evidence. If the Easter gospel is not true, all the rest falls apart. Take the risen Christ out of the NT and the rest of the story is meaningless tragedy.

In his *The Confession of an Octogenarian*, L. P. Jacks, himself a Unitarian, tells of his "discovery of the New Testament" when he was well over fifty (pp. 226 ff.). He reread the NT, not in fragments, but a whole book, Epistle, or Gospel, at a sitting. The central theme of the NT as he then rediscovered it was resurrection, "the immortality of the believer in Christ as risen from the dead."

> Sometimes in the foreground with the light full on it (as in 1 Corinthians 15), sometimes in the middle distance, sometimes in the background; but its presence, whether in one position or another, always the unifying element, holding the parts together and making of the New Testament a unitary whole. [P. 229]

Just because this is so universally the NT theme, it is interesting to find that in the Gospel accounts the acceptance of the resurrection of Jesus is at first hesitant and tentative. In today's Gospel, for example, Luke informs us that the news of the women returning from the tomb struck the apostles as "an idle tale, and they did not believe them." Both Matthew and Mark record the same kind of reaction.

Of course! In a world dominated by hell and death, this news is too good, this mighty act of God is too great to fit in with our common human experience. It is the story of Israel at the Red Sea all over again. Who could possibly believe such a story? Really it is only in the light of the rest of the NT—the changed lives, the new community, the continuing presence of the Lord by the Spirit—that the story becomes believable.

All of that will develop as the lections proceed through the Easter season. On Easter morning it is the sheer proclamation of the unexpected victory of God in the resurrection of Jesus Christ from the dead that is the business of Christian preaching.

Two themes emerge from the day's lessons. The first is that the resurrection is God's yes to man's no. The cross was our strident no to all of the demands of God for love and obedience. We showed what we thought of them, and, mind you, it was not hooligans and dope addicts who showed it, but the very best and noblest of human achievements. It was Hebrew religion and Roman justice that nailed him there, symbolizing not the worst but the best in human existence. Our human best said no at the cross, and obviously meant it.

But three days later, God said yes to all that we had denied. In the resurrection of Jesus Christ from the dead, he gave eternal validation to the very things we thought we were finally rid of. What we had denied he now affirms as the bedrock stuff of the universe. In the resurrection of our Lord, love, forgiveness, reconciliation, trust, hope—they all arise to eternal life and eternal validity.

That is why Paul can say in today's Second Lesson that the gospel of the resurrection is the gospel "in which you stand, by which you are saved." For if Jesus Christ is not risen from the dead, then all of the things in which we want to believe and by which we want to live are wildly romantic guesses with no chance of fulfillment. There is no way out; we are still in our sins. But if the resurrection is true, then a whole new world is possible.

The Resurrection of Our Lord

In his book *The Everlasting Man*, G. K. Chesterton somewhere says that when the women came early in the morning to anoint the body, not even they realized that it was really the world that had died in the night. But that's actually true. The resurrection of Jesus means the death of all the ways in which the world has traditionally worked, the death of all the values in terms of which the world has lived. Easter is the first day of a whole new creation.

The second theme grows closely out of the first. It is what might be called the *ethics of Easter*. Paul puts it clearly at the end of his long discussion of the resurrection in 1 Corinthians 15. Therefore (because Jesus Christ is risen from the dead, because resurrection is also your hope) "be steadfast, immovable, always abounding in the work of the Lord, knowing that in the Lord your labor is not in vain."

In other words, it is possible for us to live out the implications of God's Easter *yes* even in a world which is still set to deny it and say *no*. We can live in his new creation even in the midst of the powers and principalities of the old—and live there with the taste of final victory even though that victory be as dark and distant as it seemed on Good Friday. Easter is not only the validation of Jesus Christ, but the validation of his people. The implications of this faith for our lives in a world of completely false values and unworthy motivations are literally staggering.

One final word. This kind of life in our kind of world is not, as it might at first seem, a matter of grim obedience. It is in fact a doxology, an act of triumphant praise. The ancient song of Moses is really as contemporary as any pop tune. Looking straight at all of the claims and constraints of the actual world in which we really live, but a world which is now seen in the light of Easter, we cannot keep the victorious song down. "I will sing to the Lord, for he has triumphed gloriously. The Lord is my strength and my song, and he has become my salvation; this is my God, and I will praise him."

Easter Evening or Easter Monday

Lutheran	Roman Catholic	Episcopal
Dan. 12:1c–3	Acts 5:12–16	Acts 2:14, 22–32
1 Cor. 5:6–8	Rev. 1:9–11a, 12–19	
Luke 24:13–49	John 20:19–31	Matt. 28:9–15

EXEGESIS

First Lesson: Dan. 12:1c–3. In the Book of Daniel we are confronted with apocalyptic literature, a type of literature that flourished in the period between the OT and the NT but which is only rarely represented in the OT itself. This type of literature is marked by five characteristics:

(1) It is strongly dualistic. It sets the present world, which has fallen under Satan's dominion, over against a coming heavenly world, where God alone will be creator and king.

(2) It is visionary-pseudonymous. The coming new world is glimpsed by a visionary—usually an old worthy of the past— who sketches a history of the world and concentrates on the last days of this world, which he predicts are breaking in during the time that he himself is living and writing.

(3) It is deterministic. The old world will come to an end at a moment which has been determined by God, and God will suddenly intervene and allow his kingdom to come.

(4) It is thus predictive in character. The writer of the apocalypse— of the "revelation" of hidden things—gives the faithful a summary of the time schedule of the end time.

(5) It is comfort literature. The faithful are at present suppressed by Satan's forces and historical enemies such as the Roman Empire, and God's justice seems to have lost out. However, soon, at the end time, there will be a complete reversal: the faithful will be rewarded; the oppressors—now seemingly victorious—will be destroyed.

It is in this context of the transmutation of all values that the apocalypticist introduces the Pharisaic doctrine of the resurrection of the dead. In the OT proper a resurrection doctrine does not exist because death is not seen as the last enemy, since man continues to live on in the prosperity of his children or tribe. But in the apocalyptic literature the resurrection of the dead insures that faithfulness will receive its ultimate reward. Since it is not rewarded on our present earth, where satanic forces rule and oppress, faithfulness to the God of Israel and his covenant will be rewarded in the kingdom of God, when "many of those who sleep in the dust of the earth shall awake, some to everlasting life and some to shame and everlasting contempt" (v. 2). Thus the resurrection serves to show that God is just and will ultimately reward faithfulness to him.

Second Lesson: 1 Cor. 5:6–8. Paul is responding to information he has received from Corinth via the people of Chloe (1:11) and via a letter with questions from the Corinthians themselves (7:1). In chap. 5 he is dealing with a case of gross immorality: it is a case of incest, in which a man is living with his father's wife. Instead of punishing this man, the Corinthian church simply tolerates his conduct. Paul calls the Corinthians' attitude another manifestation of boasting (5:6) and thus relates it to the nature of the religiosity of the Corinthians. They believe that as a result of Christ's death and resurrection they already participate spiritually in Christ's new heavenly life. And since this individualistic spiritual heavenly life is all that matters, the things and issues of this world are no longer important. Since the Corinthians reject a resurrection of *the body*, all affairs concerning the body and concrete moral life in this world no longer matter; all that matters is spiritual completion (4:8, 9).

Since the Jewish Passover feast is close at hand when Paul is writing, he uses the Passover symbolism of unleavened bread and the Passover lamb to remind the Corinthians of their moral obligations and the newness of life which participation in Christ involves.

Thus the unleavened bread which Israel eats at its Passover is used to illustrate for the church as the new Israel the difference between the pre-Christian life of the Corinthians and their present Christian status. "Cleanse out the old leaven that you may be a new lump, as you really are unleavened. For Christ, *our* paschal lamb, has been sacrificed" (5:7). Since Christ has been sacrificed for us, we, participating in him, have already become unleavened bread in him. On the basis of this indicative of salvation, we can now live our lives in terms of a new moral imperative: leave the old leaven of your past, with all its immoral actions, urges Paul, and behave in the totality of your life like the unleavened bread of the new life—the life of sincerity and truth.

Gospel: Luke 24:13-49. The basic sections of Luke 24 have already been outlined above (see p. 3). Luke 24:13-49 is comprised of the second section of the chapter (vv. 13-35), the appearance of the risen Lord to the two disciples on the Emmaus road, and most of the third section (vv. 36-49), the appearance of Christ in the upper room. It does not include vv. 50-53 which report Christ's ascension and which can be seen either as a conclusion to the third section—the ascension is the climax to the postresurrection appearances—or as an independent fourth section. The ascension is clearly reported in Luke's second volume, the Book of Acts, where Christ's forty-day stay prior to the ascension, which Luke 24 does not report, is described.

The second section, the Emmaus story (vv. 13-35), is one of the most beautiful resurrection stories in the NT. Nothing harsh or crude about the resurrection is found here. The story centers on two pivotal points: it is a recognition story and it is a story in which Christ himself becomes the interpreter of the Scriptures, that is, the interpreter of God's salvation history which climaxes in his own death and resurrection; cf. v. 27: "And beginning with Moses and all the prophets, he interpreted to them in all the scriptures the things concerning himself." In the third section we meet Christ again as the interpreter of Scripture (v. 45). Yet, although the two disciples have the Scriptures opened to them by Christ and although they later report that their hearts burned within them while Christ did so, he remained a stranger to them until "he was known to them in the breaking of the bread" (v. 35). In other words, recognition is not based on miraculous happenings as in the third section, where Christ has the disciples touch him and proves the reality of his bodily presence by eating fish. It occurs rather in a eucharistic setting: Christ's resurrection is seen, as in the Last Supper, in the light of the death Jesus died for many. Thus the resurrection here confirms the lasting significance of Jesus' Last Supper, and of his death as a new covenant for the disciples.

In the following scene the recognition of Christ is described in a much more material and physical way. Luke intends to ban the impression that Christ's resurrection body is a spooky apparition; he intends to say that the risen Christ is identical with the rabbi Jesus. He thus combats a view which would stress an essential difference between a spiritual Christ essence and the historical Jesus.

But even in our section the story does not center so much on the fact

Easter Evening or Easter Monday

of the resurrection as on its significance. Its significance rests on the fact that Jesus' resurrection is the fulfillment of Scripture (vv. 44–46) and that it is the foundation for a universal gospel of repentance and forgiveness of sins, a gospel which offers the nations a new life.

HOMILETICAL INTERPRETATION

At first sight, it is difficult to see any real connection between these three lessons, except for the general Easter theme. The short passage from Daniel is one of the very few references anywhere in the OT to the life of the world to come. The brief cutting from Paul's first letter to the Corinthians, while it reinforces the parallel between Passover and Easter, is in fact an exhortation to Christians to live out the implications of Easter. The story in Luke's Gospel is the marvelous one about the walk to Emmaus on Easter afternoon, the recognition in the breaking of bread and the subsequent results in Jerusalem.

We shall begin with the Gospel. Whatever one may make of the story, it is impossible to overlook the strong eucharistic overtones in the scene at the inn (vv. 30–31). Although Luke had no awareness of the unhappy battles which would later divide and fragment the church, he had a strong awareness of the eucharist as a means by which the living Christ confronts his own.

One of our great problems with the eucharist, especially in Western Christianity, has been the almost exclusive way in which we have identified it with Good Friday. "This do in remembrance of me," coupled with some of Paul's statements, has been our way of approach to the supper, a way that strongly emphasizes the crucified Christ.

Without passing any judgment on that way, we need to know that there is another way, a way that connects the sacrament with Easter. It is the living Christ who makes himself known in the breaking of the bread, who eats and drinks with his own, who uses the sacramental action to make them gloriously aware of his risen and conquering presence. In this way, what often tends to be gloomy and lugubrious among us can become a joyful and exhilarating experience.

Indeed, looking at the whole story in Luke, it can be seen as a kind of prototype of the act of worship as Christians have always understood it. Here at the center is the joyful supper, but it was preceded by that long walk in which he opened to them the Scriptures, just as the proclamation of the word precedes the breaking of the bread in our worship and is an essential part of it.

The Christian church has argued endlessly about the real presence of Christ in the supper, but only recently has it begun to be serious about the real presence of Christ in his word. Yet in Luke's story, he is, to use our language, both preacher and celebrant. It was he who "interpreted to them in all the scriptures the things concerning himself." That is exactly what a sermon still ought to be—not a read essay on some vaguely religious topic, but an interpretation of the words of the Bible which reveals the living Word made flesh.

But Luke clearly indicates a third element in worship which the church has all too generally forgotten. No sooner had the two travelers to Emmaus had their burning hearts confirmed by the realization of the presence than they took off for Jerusalem to share their experience with the still hesitant and uncertain disciples. In other words, mission is as essential an element in worship as word and sacrament. Church services which end with the benediction (as all too often they do) are dangerously incomplete. If they do not result in telling what has happened and in sharing the presence, they are really a form of selfish idolatry.

It is from that perspective that we now look at Paul's exhortation to his friends in Corinth. What is the festival which he is urging them to keep? Certainly it is not the Jewish Passover, nor is it even the Christian Easter. The imagery is complex, but clearly the festival is nothing less than the new life in Christ. Even as at the Jewish Passover, all the old leaven was cleared out and a wholly new start made in baking, so Christians are to make a complete break with the old ways and the old values and start all over again with a new way of life.

"In sincerity and truth" (v. 8): The force of Paul's words hardly comes through in the English translation. First of all we need to notice that his "celebrate" (v. 8a) is a verb of continuous action bearing out the contention that it is the whole Christian life which is the festival. But "sincerity" really does not tell us what Paul had in mind. What he is talking about is commitment to the moral character of Jesus Christ which is unspotted by any deviation or compromise. And "truth" means *reality,* the way God's world really is because now we see God's world in the light of the risen Christ.

So our Christian lives are a celebration, a joyful experience of commitment to what is real, to the reality displayed in the life and death of our Lord and validated by his resurrection. The new life in Christ is not a slight improvement on the old, but something totally different which is now possible for us because Christ has brought us over from the old world to the new.

And certainly we need to remember that one of the great motifs in this new style of life is the hope that in God's love and mercy it will continue beyond the experience of death. It is not that by celebrating the festival of new life we can buy our way into heaven, but that our new life has qualities which are greater than death. Notice that in the Daniel passage it is not only the "wise" who shall "shine like the brightness of the firmament," but also those "who turn many to righteousness."

Certainly the Christian experience, the experience of the Emmaus travelers when they returned to Jerusalem, is implicit in this OT text. Wisdom and righteousness are not self-contained virtues; they are styles of life which can finally be measured only in terms of the way in which they are persuasively shared. For too long in the Christian cause we have been hung up on private goodness and morality. Insofar as there is still an ethical strain in contemporary Christianity, this is the way it goes—keeping our own selves pure in the midst of a naughty world.

Well, that is not to be despised, but it is only a beginning, a beginning which, incidentally, has been achieved by many of the world's moral teachers. What is different about the Christian style is the way in which it sends our private morality out in scores of directions in which it can be usefully and persuasively shared with others. There is little or no festival in the morality of *Poor Richard's Almanac* which so often has been misunderstood as the ethic of the gospel. But the morality that spends itself lavishly so that others can live abundantly contains continual celebration.

In our day it has become popular to omit from that celebration anything that refers to life beyond this life. Perhaps that omission has been a necessary corrective of what was in much Christian practice an overemphasis. Certainly it is a motif which does not occupy whole pages of the NT. But just as certainly it is a motif the omission of which does violence to the message of the NT. Daniel's vision is part of the picture; the ultimate victory of Christ's kingdom of holy and righteous love is essential to the gospel. Our hope, as Paul says, is for more than this life only—or we are miserable men indeed!

From the Emmaus walk to the final resurrection is not such a long distance after all, for between them lies the festival of the new life in Christ. After all, it was with enthusiastic joy that those two travelers ran back to the city to spread the good news. For them life had been changed from a dreary "we had so hoped" to the warmth of the burning heart. In their experience we ought to be able to see a parable of our own as we are continually confronted by the risen Christ in Scripture and sacrament, in breaking of bread, and joyfully commit ourselves to sharing the news until his kingdom has fully come and the world for which he died at last belongs to him.

The Second Sunday of Easter

Lutheran	*Roman Catholic*	*Episcopal*	*Presbyterian and UCC*
Acts 8:26–40	Acts 5:12–16	Acts 5:12–16	Acts 5:12–16
Rev. 1:9–19	Rev. 1:9–19	Rev. 1:4–10a, 12–18	Rev. 1:9–13, 17–19
John 20:19–31	John 20:19–31	John 20:19–31	John 21:1–14

EXEGESIS

First Lesson: Acts 8:26–40. This section of the Book of Acts gives us a clear indication that the promise of the risen Lord, first recorded in Luke 24 and then in Acts 1, is being realized. In Luke 24:45 the risen Lord "said to them: 'Thus it is written that the Christ should suffer and on the third day rise from the dead, and that repentance and forgiveness of sins should be preached in his name to all nations, beginning from Jerusalem.'" In Acts 1:8 the apostles' commission is stated even more clearly: "You shall receive power when the Holy Spirit has come upon you and you shall be my witnesses in Jerusalem and in all Judea and Samaria and to the end of the earth."

Acts 8 now records the spread of the gospel from Jerusalem into Judea and Samaria and to the end of the earth. The chapter is mainly concerned with Philip's preaching in Samaria and with the conversion and deceit of Simon, the magician; it ends with the command of the angel of the Lord (v. 26) or with that of the Spirit (vv. 29, 39) to Philip to travel south to Philistia and join the chariot of the Ethiopian finance minister.

The Second Sunday of Easter

Thereby the spread of the gospel to Ethiopia is clearly suggested, since it is reported that although the eunuch saw Philip no more, he was baptized and "went on his way rejoicing" (v. 39).

Philip was one of the deacons, appointed by the Twelve to serve tables in Acts 6:1-7. His basic activity seems to have been that of an evangelist. In Acts 21:8-9 we encounter him again as an evangelist; he is living in Caesarea with four unmarried daughters who prophesy.

Although the Holy Spirit had been given to the disciples on Pentecost, the Spirit is, as it were, the gift of the resurrection and is closely associated with it. For the Holy Spirit takes the place of the now ascended Lord and empowers the apostles and their company to be on the move with the gospel throughout the world. Thus, in our section, the Spirit, represented as a personal force at times, enables Philip to do three things: (1) He moves the evangelist to new missionary tasks. (2) He enables the evangelist to interpret Scripture, just as the risen Lord had done with his disciples in Luke 24. Philip now interprets Isaiah 53 to the Ethiopian as having been fulfilled in the cross and resurrection of Jesus (v. 35). (3) The Spirit is probably connected here with the power of baptism.

As soon as Philip has baptized the eunuch, the Spirit moves him to new territory: "the Spirit of the Lord caught up Philip . . . Philip was found at Azotus, and passing on he preached the gospel to all the towns till he came to Caesarea" (vv. 39, 40).

Second Lesson: Rev. 1:9-19. It is appropriate that the Easter cycle of biblical passages should concentrate not only on the resurrection stories, but also on the responsibility of the churches for the resurrection message. The Revelation of John is the only full-fledged piece of apocalyptic literature in the NT. It is similar to the Book of Daniel in the OT except for two important changes: in the first place, whereas most apocalyptic literature is anonymous, the apocalyptist here speaks and writes in his own name: "John to the seven churches that are in Asia" (1:4). In the second place, apocalyptic literature is wholly directed toward the future, toward "what must soon take place" (1:1). However, in this apocalypse the specifically Christian element lies in the fact that the future has already been opened up by what has taken place, namely, the event of "Jesus Christ the faithful witness, the firstborn of the dead and the ruler of kings on earth" (1:5).

Rev. 1:9–19 deals with the apocalyptic preface to the letters to the seven churches of Asia Minor, which comprise the first three chapters of the book. In these verses John tells how he went into a trance, probably in the midst of a worship service, and had auditory and visionary experiences: "I was in the Spirit on the Lord's day, and I heard behind me a loud voice. . . . Then I turned to see the voice . . . and on turning I saw seven golden lampstands" (1:10–12). John, who lives in exile on the island of Patmos because of the Christian witness, is commanded in the trance to write to the seven churches of Asia Minor. He is to write in the name of the Risen One, who is portrayed as an austere judge, "one like a son of man . . . his eyes were like a flame of fire, his feet were like burnished bronze," etc. (1:14–15). It is the Risen One who is rising to the last judgment in order to pronounce his churches faithful or faithless to him.

Therefore, *resurrection* is both a word of promise—of ultimate victory over end and death—but also a word of judgment, if the church fails to remain faithful to the word of the gospel and fails to carry on its life in accord with that word. So Sardis must hear: "I know your works; you have the name of being alive and you are dead" (3:1), and Laodicea must hear: "I know your works; you are neither cold nor hot. Would that you were cold or hot. So because you are lukewarm and neither cold nor hot, I will spew you out of my mouth." On the other hand Ephesus may hear: "I know your works, your toil and your patient endurance . . . I know you are enduring patiently and bearing up for my name's sake and you have not grown weary" (2:2, 3). Thus *resurrection* means Gospel message and eternal life, but it also means responsibility and faithfulness, without which one will be rejected by the judgment of the coming Risen One.

Gospel: John 20:19–31. As was the case with Luke 24, so John 20 should be read and considered in its entirety. Essentially it comprises three sections: (1) Vv. 1–10: the running of Peter and the beloved disciple to the tomb. (2) Vv. 11–18: Jesus' appearance to Mary Magdalene at the empty tomb. (3) Vv. 19–31: Jesus' appearance to the disciples and Thomas.

Within the third section there are three subsections: (1) Vv. 19–23: Jesus' appearance to the disciples. (2) Vv. 24–29: Jesus' appearance to Thomas. (3) Vv. 30–31: The conclusion of the Gospel of John as a whole.

(1) Vv. 19–23: This section briefly narrates Jesus' appearance, the missionary charge to the disciples, and the gift of the Spirit which both prepares the disciples for their missionary work and endows them with apostolic authority. This apostolic authority enables them to forgive or retain sins. We should notice that what is stretched out over a longer period in the Book of Acts is coalesced here. The tunes of Easter and Pentecost are intermingled, as it were. This makes it possible to locate Pentecost on Easter and to locate there as well the missionary and ecclesiastical endowments of the disciples. Besides, the Spirit does not fall from heaven on the disciples in the dramatic manner of Acts 2, but it is given, "breathed" by Jesus himself (v. 22).

(2) Vv. 24–29: The story of Thomas is well known. Thomas needs empirical evidence in order to come to faith. Yet the climax of the story is meant to discredit this type of faith; the readers of the Gospel are to heed the words "Blessed are those who have not seen and yet believe" (v. 29).

From another angle the confession of Thomas is a climax to which the Gospel as such has led: "My Lord and my God" (v. 28). This confession constitutes our proper relationship to Jesus, and it is this confession of Jesus as Lord and God which was the underlying purpose of the Gospel as a whole.

(3) Vv. 30–31: We might have expected these concluding words of the Gospel at the close of the Book of Signs (chaps. 2–12). Generally scholars have detected six or seven signs in John: the changing of water into wine in Cana (chap. 2); the healing of the officer's son (chap. 4); Bethesda (chap. 5); the bread miracle (chap. 6); the healing of the man born blind (chap. 9); the raising of Lazarus (chap. 11); and the crucifixion as the seventh or complete sign. The reference to signs in v. 30 makes us think that the climax to all the other signs was the miracle of the resurrection appearance. However that may be, the purpose behind the Gospel of John comes to light here: "that you believe that Jesus is the Christ, the Son of God, and that believing you may have life in his name."

HOMILETICAL INTERPRETATION

If thus far we have stressed the importance of Christ risen rather than Christ crucified, it has not been to establish a polarity between them, but rather to establish their identity. It is that identity and the necessity for maintaining it that is the common thread which unites the three lections for this first Sunday after Easter.

To begin with John's vision in Revelation, the appurtenances of that vision are all those of incredible magnificence, such magnificence as defies any human conceptualizing. How could we depict one who in his golden ambience has eyes of fire, feet of burnished bronze, a face like the noonday sun and a voice like the sound of many waters? Obviously we are dealing with someone whose existence far transcends humanity.

But against that depiction must be placed what this Being says of himself. "I died, and behold I am alive forevermore" (v. 18). In a word, this transcendent Being with all power in his hands is the same Jesus who was tormented, mistreated, and finally crucified. The place of final decision and power is occupied by the very one whose lips drew human breath and whose feet walked human pathways. The crucified Jesus is the omnipotent Christ.

And it is he who holds all of the keys to the future. Not only are death and hades open to him, but the entire future, all of the things that shall occur hereafter. The same Jesus who was crucified is the Lord of history.

What this means is that because of Easter we know who is in ultimate control of human history. He is not some distant and unknowable deity, a life force or an impersonal being. Nor is the center of our gospel anything so feeble as the spirit of a noble, misunderstood martyr who lost his life in a hopeless cause. The ends of the paradox are indeed staggering, but Easter enables us to hold on to both of them. The Jesus who endured all human experience, even the last and most terrifying of all, is also the Lord Christ who has the key to the future.

Perhaps the connection between this vision and Philip's experience with the Ethiopian official riding home from Jerusalem is not immediately apparent. It was the celebrated "suffering servant" passage in Isaiah 53 that the official was reading as he was being driven home. He was puzzled to know to whom it was that the prophet was referring, as indeed are many persons who do not have the benefit of an interpreter.

But you will notice, Philip did not merely tell him that the reference was to Jesus. The author of Acts makes it clear that the identification was only Philip's starting point (v. 35). The "good news of Jesus" which he told the Ethiopian as he rode with him had to include the story of the resurrection and a testimony to the power of the living Lord. Otherwise, why would the stranger have requested baptism? In other words, Philip's identification of the suffering servant was only the starting point for his proclamation of the servant who is now the Lord.

We might pause here long enough to notice also something which we have already seen in the hasty return of the two travelers from Emmaus—an overwhelming desire to share the news of the resurrection. By this time, it has gone far beyond the bounds of the little apostolic company, has, in fact, begun to break out of the limits of the city of Jerusalem in which the event first took place and was known. But the important thing to notice is that the "sheep led to the slaughter" and the "lamb before its shearer" is not just the man Jesus, but the living Lord.

John's account of the experience of Thomas has usually been presented as the classic case of skepticism, and "doubting Thomas" has become a common English expression. But we need to do a little thinking as to the reason for Thomas's questioning attitude. The print of the nails and the scar in the side of the risen Lord were for Thomas the key question. Does this not indicate that identity was the crucial matter for the apostle? Some celestial phantom, totally different from the man of Calvary, simply would not do. The risen Lord speaking peace and empowering forgiveness *had* to be the same person who had been lifted up on the cross, or, so far as Thomas was concerned, the whole thing fell apart. If his death is not an eternal part of the living Lord, then our redemption is flawed.

Thomas's answering confession, "My Lord and my God" (v. 28), was possible only because he was convinced that the Christ of Calvary and the Christ of Easter were the same. Long centuries ago in discussing the incarnation Athanasius said, "What has not been assumed has not been redeemed." Though the language is far from that of Thomas, the thought is the same. He is our Lord and God only because he still carries the evidence of the darkest marks of our disgrace.

For Thomas it was possible to make that identification with his physical sight. For us it is not possible; nevertheless, "Blessed are those who have not seen and yet believe" (v. 29). Happy are those who are able to see in the good news of the gospel both the Jesus of the cross and the Christ of the resurrection. Happy are those who are able to keep in their gospel both the theology of the cross and the theology of glory.

Even though we may not know them by those titles, we live in a time when these two aspects of the gospel are in continual danger of flying apart. On the one hand, we have the activists whose commitment is to the ethic of the gospel and the grimness of the cross. On the other hand, we have a popular Christianity in which everything is light and glory. Both are dangerous falsifications. The NT never underestimates the grimness of the cross, but it always interprets its Good Fridays in the light of Easter. Just as certainly, the NT always connects the power of the resurrection with the fellowship in the suffering.

What binds these two apparently disparate elements together in the NT is, of course, the figure of Jesus the Lord, the man of sorrows who is the king of glory, the exalted king who was the servant obedient to death. It is essential for the integrity of our gospel that he be the same. We have no need for one more tragic martyr; we have had too many already. Their repetition simply deepens our despair. Certainly we have no need for a divinity untouched by our human agony. What could he possibly know of our situation? What could he do for it?

No, our need has been beautifully described in Jennet's speech in Christopher Fry's play, *The Lady's Not for Burning* (p. 83):

> . . . Then if time and space
> Have any purpose, I shall belong to it.
> If not, if all is a pretty fiction
> To distract the cherubim and seraphim
> Who so continually do cry, the least
> I can do is to fill the curled shell of the world
> With human deep-sea sound, and hold it to
> The ear of God, until he has appetite
> To taste our salt sorrow on his lips.

That was how Thomas felt; he was tired of pretty fictions, as all of us are. But the good news is that in Jesus Christ God *has* tasted our salt sorrow on his lips, and that the same Jesus who did that bitter tasting is the king who holds the key to all of our futures. The deep-sea sound with which he cried, "My God, My God, why hast Thou forsaken me?" was spoken with the voice of him who now addresses evil, hell, and death with a voice like the sound of many waters. That's the good news.

How much we need to enlarge our understanding of Easter! Instead of being an annual festival, it is the groundtone of our entire gospel. It is Easter that puts together all of the parts of the NT. There is a direct relationship between the Sermon on the Mount and the final judgment, a direct relationship between the miracles of healing and the church's life in the world, a direct relationship between the death on Calvary and the glorious Lord of life. Behold, I was dead and now I am alive for evermore. My Lord and my God!

The Third Sunday of Easter

Lutheran	Roman Catholic	Episcopal	Presbyterian and UCC
Acts 5:27–42	Acts 5:27b–32, 40b–41	Acts 5:27–35	Acts 5:27–32
Rev. 5:11–14	Rev. 5:11–14	Rev. 5:6–14	Rev. 5:11–14
John 21:1–14	John 21:1–19	John 21:1–14	John 21:15–19

EXEGESIS

First Lesson: Acts 5:27–42. This section could be called "the resurrection in action." For "preaching Jesus as the Christ" (5:42) means giving public witness to the resurrection as vv. 30 f. have it: "The God of our fathers raised Jesus whom you killed by hanging him on a tree. God exalted him at his right hand as Leader and Savior, to give repentance to Israel and forgiveness of sins." Apostolic preaching, then, is preaching of the resurrection, supported by the gift of the Holy Spirit (v. 32) and by signs of healing (vv. 15, 16). The core of this section deals with the words of Gamaliel, who warns the council not to interfere too hastily with the business of the apostles: "if it [this undertaking] is of God, you will not be able to overthrow them. You might even be found opposing God." In other words, the section shows that the acts of the apostles are really the acts of God; therefore, no human force can resist the victorious march of the gospel through the world. Thus our section places before us the theme of all of Acts: the providential and victorious march of the gospel through the world, reaching its climax when in chap. 28 the center of that world, Rome, the capital, is reached.

This theme of the victorious march of the gospel could be undergirded by a second theme, namely, the theme that Tertullian summed up with the words: "The blood of the martyrs is the seed of the church." For despite, or rather because of suffering, the gospel is victorious. V. 41 states this theme as follows: "Then they left the presence of the council, rejoicing that they were counted worthy to suffer dishonor for the name." Our section thus indicates the collision of church and world, the hostility which missionary activity evokes in the world. Immediately after their miraculous release from prison (vv. 19 ff.), the apostles go to the temple to preach the power of Jesus' name (vv. 20, 25; cf. 3:16). Arrested once more, they give their testimony to the high priest and the Sanhedrin and again we are struck by the courage and boldness of their testimony (vv. 29–32; cf. 4:13 f., 33).

The council's plan to murder the apostles is thwarted by the wise counsel of Gamaliel, a pupil of Hillel, who was the leader of the more moderate rabbinic school. Gamaliel appeals to the providence of God. Once this is accepted, the apostles disregard the charge to stop preaching and instead, "every day in the temple and at home they did not cease teaching and preaching Jesus as the Christ" (v. 42).

Take notice that the author of Acts has Gamaliel misdate the activities of Theudas and Judas. Both Judas the Galilean and Theudas were Zealots. Judas tried to prevent the census under Quirinius in A.D. 6 and Theudas intended to cross the Jordan river with followers under the procurator Cuspius Fadus, ca. A.D. 46, obviously to enact a second Red Sea miracle and to march up in order to free Jerusalem from Roman rule.

Second Lesson: Rev. 5:11–14. This section is the climax of the mighty opening scene of the actual "apocalypse" or "revelation" of John. The first three chapters of the Book of Revelation are devoted to the seven churches of Asia Minor, to praise, blame, and exhort them. Chap. 4 sets the scene of the "revelation" and describes the mighty throne of God, the creator and judge, surrounded by the four animals, the seven spirits of God, and the twenty-four elders on their thrones. Chap. 5 describes the scroll, "written within and on the back, sealed with seven seals" (v. 1), which nobody is considered worthy enough to open.

Here we are suddenly introduced to the christological center of the revelation, for at once there appears a lamb and the despair of the seer is taken away. "Weep not; lo, the Lion of the tribe of Judah, the Root of David has conquered, so that he can open the scroll and its seven seals" (v. 5). The lamb now is worshiped and glorified and the christological center of the revelation points to an eschatological climax. The Lamb, although slain, is worshiped as the king of creation by the unanimous voice of all creatures "in heaven and on earth and under the earth and

The Third Sunday of Easter

in the sea" (v. 13). Thus before the revelation begins to unfold the horrible scenes of the end time with its trials and martyrdoms, the victory of the Lamb can nevertheless be celebrated, because "Worthy is the Lamb who was slain, to receive power and wealth and wisdom and might and honor and glory and blessing!" (v. 12).

Notwithstanding the coming tribulations and the eschatological trials, the victory of God has been already established, because the glorious resurrection of the Lamb has already taken place. It is a witness to the centrality of Christ that even an apocalypse, mainly devoted to future happenings, can point to a center in which these future happenings have already been predetermined and anticipated. It is a striking paradox that amid all the animalistic images of the resurrection, it is a lamb—even a slain lamb—who is worshiped as the secret meaning and center of all victory.

Gospel: John 21:1-14. There is general consensus among scholars that John 21 is an appendix to the Gospel of John. There is, however, disagreement about whether it was written by the author of the Gospel or by a member of the Johannine school. Vocabulary and style are quite Johannine.

It is noteworthy that the setting of this postresurrection appearance in John 21 is Galilean, whereas the body of the Gospel locates the resurrection appearances firmly in Jerusalem and in Jerusalem alone. John 21 therefore continues the tradition of Galilean resurrection appearances as foretold by Mark and substantiated by Matthew. Since John 20:30, 31 plainly constitutes the end and climax of the Gospel, John 21 is clearly an addendum.

The chapter has often been compared with Luke 5:1-11, where a miraculous catch of fish is also reported and where the disciples are called to become fishers of men. Although John 21 does not spell this out, the sequence in vv. 15 ff., where Peter is exhorted, "Feed my lambs," "Tend my sheep" and "Feed my sheep," suggests a possible link between the miraculous catch of fish and the calling of the disciples to feed the flock of the church.

The story takes place in Galilee. It seems as if no prior resurrection appearance has taken place in Jerusalem and as if the great commission to the disciples and the gift of the Spirit (John 20:21-23) have not yet been given. After the crucifixion the disciples seem simply to have returned to their former occupations as fishermen. That night they had poor luck and caught nothing (cf. Luke 5:5). But suddenly at dawn a stranger calls to them from the beach: "Children, have you any fish?" Upon their negative reply, the stranger commands them to cast the net on the right side of the boat, and the miraculous catch takes place. Again it is the beloved disciple who, as in the story of the empty tomb (John 20:8), gains the first insight. Then he tells Peter, "It is the Lord" (v. 7).

The scene now shifts from fishing to a eucharistic setting, which in the story is called a breakfast. Eucharistic overtones are clearly present: "Jesus came and took the bread and gave it to them, and so with the fish" (v. 13). Notice that the author calls this the third resurrection appearance to the disciples (v. 14), thereby attempting to link chap. 21 to chap. 20, just as the "again" of v. 1 serves this purpose.

HOMILETICAL INTERPRETATION

It must seem a long distance spatially, temporally, and conceptually from the ten thousand times ten thousand with their triumphant hymn of praise, "Worthy is the Lamb who was slain" to a courtroom in Jerusalem in which the judges have to deal with men who refuse to be silent but insist on publicly spreading disturbing news. Because of the immortal music to which Handel set the heavenly song in his *Messiah*, we feel somewhat familiar with the words sung in that celestial setting, but there is little else, if anything, in the rest of the scene in Revelation with which we can identify or feel at home.

The story from Acts, however, is one which has had so many parallels in our time that we feel much at home with it. While there was more at stake, at the very least Peter and the apostles are involved in a NT case of civil disobedience. "We must obey God rather than men" (v. 29) has been the confession of countless Christians from their time to our own. One could only wish that in American society there had been similar Gamaliels to deal wisely with our cases of civil disobedience rather than the sad story of barbarity and even murder which has so often greeted them.

It has often been noted that in Phil. 3:10 when Paul speaks about the necessity of knowing Christ, he places knowing the power of his resurrection before sharing in his sufferings. Logically it may seem that the

The Third Sunday of Easter

order should be reversed, but in real Christian experience Paul's order is correct.

Certainly the apostles found it so in this story. They knew the power of their Lord's resurrection; that was what they were trying to proclaim in Jerusalem, what they did proclaim fearlessly before the face of the council itself. It was for that proclamation that they were beaten (v. 40). But because they did know the power of the resurrection, they did not become bitter or vengeful or complaining. No, they rejoiced that "they were counted worthy to suffer dishonor for the name" (v. 41). Unhappily many times when we encounter stiff opposition for what we believe is a righteous cause, we do not react in the same way because we try to go from suffering to resurrection and not from resurrection to suffering. We can disobey men and do it joyfully when we do it as a part of our commitment to the new life in Christ.

But now, can you hear even a slight echo of the heavenly chorus in the defiant assertion of Peter and the apostles? Surely we need not be Calvinists to understand John Calvin's often repeated assertion that obedience is the only sure way by which men can give glory to God! It takes no real commitment to join in singing Handel's "Worthy Is the Lamb," stirring as the music is. But it takes a deep knowledge of the power of his resurrection to be able to stand up in a bitterly hostile situation and say, "We must obey God rather than men." Yet that is only another way, probably the only way that is open to us in the limitations and ambiguities of human existence, to say "Worthy is the Lamb" and mean it.

In the heavenly places where there are no shadows and no darkness at all it is possible to say "Worthy is the Lamb" and mean it because there intention and action are one. But here on earth where chasms are always opening between intention and action, the confession has to be validated by action. And the suffering which so often results from such action is simply a deeper and more significant way of saying "Worthy is the Lamb." That is why Peter and his companions took their beating with joy. It was not masochism, but genuine delight in sharing in the sufferings of their Lord that enabled them even in that situation to lift up their hearts in thanksgiving.

The late Albert Camus once said that what this world needs is people who are not afraid to speak up plainly and pay up personally. Given Camus's distrust of the church, it is not likely that he had Christians in mind when he said that. But given also the full dimensions of NT Christianity, who ought better to fit his description than the followers of Jesus Christ, able to share the sufferings because they know the power of the resurrection? Even while the church above ceases not to cry, "Worthy is the Lamb," the church below must continue to say, "We must obey God rather than men," and take the consequences. In either case, the song is the same.

The Gospel lesson continues with the same stress on obedience. Frustrated by the bewildering sequence of events since Good Friday, Peter seeks some kind of comfort in the only thing he really understands—a fishing trip. It is while he and his companions are involved in that very (for them) common activity, that they become aware of a mysterious presence on the shore offering them directions. It would have been easy for Peter to have told the stranger to mind his own business. After all, fishing was Peter's business and he didn't need some landsman telling him how to do it!

But there was something compelling about the stranger which forced Peter to listen—with amazing results. Notice, however, that Peter's response came before his full recognition. Only after the nets were full, only after John had cried, "It is the Lord," did Peter plunge into the water and start swimming for the shore. One is reminded of those memorable lines of Albert Schweitzer:

> As one unknown and nameless He comes to us, just as on the shore of the lake He approached those men who knew not who He was. His words are the same: "Follow thou Me!" and He puts us to the tasks which He has to carry out in our age. He commands. And to those who obey, be they wise or simple, He will reveal Himself through all that they are privileged to experience in His fellowship of peace and activity, of struggle and suffering, till they come to know, as an inexpressible secret, Who He is. [*Out of My Life and Thought*, pp. 48–49]

Perhaps it is also worth pointing out that Peter's call to obey came right in the midst of his ordinary life's situation. It was not in a liturgical situation, not even in a juncture of affairs that called for some heroism, as was the case with the story in Acts. Peter was fishing, and that was his livelihood. Much as it might happen to one of us at an office desk or by a machine in a factory, Peter's call to obey came while he was trying to earn a living.

We can go one step more and point out that the call to obey came not in highly religious terms, but in terms of the occupation itself. "Cast the net on the right side of the boat" (v. 6). Very often it is the decisions made in the ordinary pursuit of our everyday careers that most deeply affect our Christian obedience. Dietrich Bonhoeffer somewhere has a word about the fact that too many of us have what he called "a God of the gaps." That is to say, we rely upon God only in those rare crises for which we feel personally insufficient.

But obedience is not only for crises; indeed, if we have not been practicing it in the everyday business of our lives, we may find ourselves incapable of it in the crises. Even as in this story, the risen Christ is present in the midst of our business, so it is also in the midst of our business that the call comes to obey him. That sanctification of our common lives about which we do so much pious talking but of which we see so little reality, is no mystery. It is made up of scores of little decisions which we consciously make in accordance with what we believe to be his will. It may be so small a thing as an attitude toward a fellow employee or the filling out of an expense sheet. But it is these little acts of obedience that build the character which someday can stand up and say, "We must obey God rather than men," and be ready to suffer for it.

A wise old saint once remarked that "faith is three parts obedience." Certainly if we wish to be related to the living Christ in more than a nominal way, it will happen only if we are ready to listen when he says, "Follow me!"

The Fourth Sunday of Easter

Lutheran	*Roman Catholic*	*Episcopal*	*Presbyterian and UCC*
Acts 13:15, 26–33	Acts 13:14, 43–52	Acts 13:15, 26–33	Acts 13:44–52
Rev. 7:9–17	Rev. 7:9, 14b–17	Rev. 7:9–17	Rev. 7:9–17
John 10:22–30	John 10:22–30	John 10:22–30	John 10:22–30

EXEGESIS

First Lesson: Acts 13:15, 26–33. This section finds Paul and Barnabas in Antioch of Pisidia in Asia Minor. They are on their so-called first missionary journey, having been sent out on their mission by prophets of their home church in Antioch of Syria. After successful missionary work in Cyprus, where the proconsul Sergius Paulus was converted, they travel via Pamphylia to Antioch of Pisidia. In accord with their missionary strategy, they first seek out the synagogue, where, besides Jews, "God fearers" are also assembled, that is, those who sympathized with Judaism without becoming full-fledged Jews by undergoing circumcision (cf. vv. 16, 26).

As was often customary with visitors, they were asked to address the congregation after the reading of the Law and the Prophets (v. 15). Our section deals with the last part of Paul's speech on this occasion. In the first part Paul rehearses the salvation history of Israel, leading up to David and the promise of a savior in the line of David. The promise of salvation has now been fulfilled in Jesus, and thus the apostles are presently preaching the promised gospel of salvation. Paul subsequently deals with the passion story of Jesus, indicating that the Jews in Jerusalem had Jesus crucified. Thereby they fulfilled unwittingly what had been prophesied about Jesus. However, "God raised him from the dead" (v. 30); this reversal by God destroys the plan of the Jews simply to do away with Jesus and constitutes the message of salvation. The proof of the resurrection lies in the living witness of those "who came up with him from Galilee to Jerusalem, who are now his witnesses to the people" (v. 31), that is, with the historical disciples.

What, then, is the content of this message of salvation? Concretely Jesus' resurrection by God means forgiveness of sins and freedom from the guilt of the law (vv. 38 ff.). Although the author of Acts has no outspoken message of atonement through the sacrifice of Jesus, he concentrates on the resurrection of Jesus, that is, on the eternal life of Jesus and God's confirmation of Jesus' ministry. For the resurrection of Jesus means a reversal of the crucifixion and is the sign of God's confirmation of Jesus' ministry and death. The meaning of the resurrection is interpreted by Psalm 2: "Thou art my Son, today I have begotten thee" (v. 33). Thus, for the author of Acts the resurrection of Jesus is the central occurrence. It means the reversal of the death of Jesus which had been effected by the cunning of men, and it means also God's adoption of Jesus as Son by his resurrection. Paul's message meets initial success and he and Barnabas are asked to return the next sabbath (v. 42).

Second Lesson: Rev. 7:9–17. This section of the Revelation of John gives us a marvelous picture of the church militant which has become

The Fourth Sunday of Easter

the church triumphant. This section contains the liturgy of the church triumphant, worshiping and praising God for the salvation which has been given and for the rescue from martyrdom, a rescue which has been gained through martyrdom itself.

It is before the throne of God and before the Lamb that the heavenly liturgy of the martyrs takes place. "A great multitude which no man could number, from every nation, from all tribes and peoples and tongues . . . clothed in white robes, with palm branches in their hands, and crying out with a loud voice, 'Salvation belongs to our God who sits upon the throne, and to the Lamb!'" (vv. 9, 10). One of the elders functions here as an interpreting angel and asks the seer: "Who are these, clothed in white robes, and whence have they come?" (v. 13). The seer requests an answer, which is granted to him.

What now follows is the most impressive example of what every apocalypse intends; here we witness the eschatological impulse to provide comfort literature in the midst of martyrdom and oppression. Because the faithful have become martyrs, who have washed their robes in the blood of the Lamb, eternal comfort and consolation will be their part. "He who sits upon the throne will shelter them with his presence" (v. 15), and finally "God will wipe away every tear from their eyes" (v. 17). All the cruelties and ambiguities of history, all the injustices suffered by the faithful on earth will ultimately be straightened out. Thus it is important for the church, now suffering from injustice and from the feeling of "How can God allow it?" to stay patient and to wait for God's final victory, which he has already foreshadowed in the victory of the Lamb, Jesus Christ.

Gospel: John 10:22–30. Jesus is in Jerusalem to attend the feast of the dedication of the temple. (This festival took place in the month Chislev—in the winter—to commemorate the rededication of the temple under Simon Maccabeus in 164 B.C.) The Jews gather around him with a question they have already repeatedly asked: "If you are the Christ, tell us plainly" (v. 24). Jesus refers as before (5:17 f., 36 f.) to his works, which he does in his Father's name, as bearing witness to his status as Son of God. Suddenly the theme of the sheep and the shepherd, with which the chapter had opened (10:1–6, 7–18), is reintroduced. The sheep hear the voice of the shepherd, and "he calls his own sheep by name and leads them out" (10:3). "He goes before them, and the sheep follow him, for they know his voice" (10:4). The same theme occurs here in our section (10:27-28): "My sheep hear my voice, and I know them, and they follow me; and I give them eternal life." Just as 10:10 draws the contrast between the thief, the hireling, and the good shepherd who lays down his life for his sheep, so 10:28 stresses that the sheep "shall never perish, and no one shall snatch them out of my hand." What follows is the preparation for the amazing christological statement of 10:30: the way Jesus deals with the sheep is equivalent to the Father's way of dealing with them, for the Father has given the sheep to Jesus. Even more: "I and the Father are one." This statement is regarded by the Jews as utter blasphemy, and they take up stones to kill him. Yet the statement "I and the Father are one" has been indirectly enunciated in several ways in the Gospel. It is the heart of the Christology of the Gospel. For what counts about Jesus is not his heroic and appealing status as a man or miracle worker. The only thing that counts is whether people see in him God's presence. All else is indifferent. Thus, what makes a sheep a sheep is the fact that it is joined to the one flock under the one shepherd. It recognizes that in Jesus' works God himself is redemptively present. "I and the Father are one" is not primarily a metaphysical statement, but a redemptive one—in Jesus' works the works of the Father manifest themselves for the salvation of man.

HOMILETICAL INTERPRETATION

One finds it difficult to believe that John, who was so very fond of finding double meanings in what appear to be purely chronological terms (e.g., 13:30: Judas "went out; and it was night"), did not intend to say something about the spiritual as well as the physical climate in Jerusalem when he began this incident by observing that "it was winter" (v. 23). It was an uncomfortable and unpleasant time both for Jesus and his hearers as they pressed him for a definite answer to their question: "If you are the Christ, tell us plainly" (v. 24).

Jesus' reply was one which he often gave to such questions. He gave it to the disciples of John the Baptist when they came asking if he was the one who was to come or whether they should look for another (cf. Matt. 11:2-6). The essence of that reply was that his works were his credentials. If anyone really perceived what he was doing, he would know that it was what his Father would do, for he and his Father were

The Fourth Sunday of Easter

one (v. 30). What intellectual, christological concept could possibly compare with this complete identity in both intention and deed?

Yet, at the same time, our Lord had sadly to admit that it was possible for men to look at these deeds and see nothing in them. The reason which he assigned for their failure was the fact that they did not belong to his sheep (v. 26). At that point, many of us probably lose sympathy because it seems to us that we are perilously close to that whole mysterious business about *election* which has so bedeviled Christian thought through the centuries. And besides that, didn't Karl Barth once say that if you scratch an American you will find someone who believes in freedom of the will?

But without getting into the mystery of election (in which our Lord quite evidently believed), it ought to be possible for us to say this much. His sheep, the ones who did accept his credentials, did so because they were already in a living relationship with him. They heard his voice and followed him; they experienced the gift of real life which he offered them (vv. 27–28). They did not stand on the outside trying to make up their minds about his claims before they became involved. They were certain of his claims because they were already involved.

Perhaps there are still those who try to make an intellectual case for the claims of Jesus Christ before they make any kind of commitment to him. That may work in a college debating society, but it is too artificial for real living. Our Lord's challenge is to get involved with the flock and then decide. "If any man's will is to do his will, he shall know whether the teaching is from God or whether I am speaking on my own authority" (7:17).

And it is just as true that once we have been involved in that kind of commitment, no one is going to change our minds, "no one is able to snatch them out of the Father's hand" (v. 29). Some clever fellow may be able to give us a bad time logically, but the real involvement between us and our Lord in so many of life's deepest concerns is far too great to be turned around all that easily. So far as we are concerned, his own best credentials are what has happened in our own lives because of his grace and his power. There is nobody who can talk us out of that. We belong and we know we belong.

Certainly when Paul spoke to the men in the synagogue in Antioch of Pisidia, this was what he was talking about. He declared to them that along with his brethren, he was a witness to the good news of the resurrection. He could not have meant that either he or they saw Jesus rise from the dead. No mortal saw that. Some of them may have seen the empty tomb, but they were very few in number.

No, when Paul spoke about being a witness to the good news of the resurrection, he was not making an intellectual argument, but using his own transformation as exhibit A. This was Saul, the man who had hated Jesus and all his works with what he believed was a holy hatred, Saul, now become Paul, the great apostle of Jesus and his love. If that was not a witness to the resurrection, what was? Once again, the work of Christ was his credentials.

An old Methodist evangelist used to tell of a little girl whose father was a converted drunkard. One of her schoolmates began to taunt her about believing in the gospel yarn that claimed that Jesus turned water into wine. "I don't know about that" she replied. "But I do know that in our house Jesus turned whiskey into water—and that's miracle enough for me!" My works are my credentials. We are witnesses of his resurrection.

If our gospel lacks persuasiveness in today's secular world, one great reason is the lack of witnesses of the resurrection, men and women whose life-styles are different because they have become involved with Jesus Christ. On a Sunday in Eastertide, we hear the story of his resurrection, go home to a chicken dinner, and pick up where we left off on Monday morning. Sunday after Sunday we are involved in the greatest event in history, but nothing ever happens to us. We have no credentials with which to display his claims, no *show and tell* part of our Christian lives.

But who were the martyrs that John saw in his vision in Revelation 7? Not bloodless stained-glass window figures, but simple men and women like you and me who even at great cost to themselves sought to be with Christ in his obedience to his Father's will. ("They have washed their robes and made them white in the blood of the Lamb," v. 14.) They were slaves and school teachers, plumbers and salesmen, housewives and hairdressers, all of whom, because they were witnesses of his resurrection, sheep of his flock, found the power to say yes when they had to say yes and no when they had to say no. They came out of all nations, all races, all classes and all cultures. Some were advantaged and some were disadvantaged. Only this one thing they had in common. The risen Jesus had been at work in their lives making them new.

The Fourth Sunday of Easter

And what is their reward? Language is a poor instrument for the description of transcendent reality, but John does his best. All of his metaphors come simply to this. Now at last they are able to do perfectly what on earth they sought to do, but now without any limitation or restraint. "They serve God day and night" (v. 15). Their tears of frustration, their dryness of spirit, their weariness of mind and body—all these are gone. They are fully in possession of the gift of self-renewing life. "The Lamb in the midst of the throne will be their shepherd, and he will guide them to springs of living water" (v. 17). In a word, the witnesses to the resurrection will see the risen Lord; the sheep will at last meet their Shepherd.

It is worth noticing how many of the pericopes for these Sundays in Eastertide include one lesson from the Revelation of John the Divine. That kind of reading has not been fashionable in the church in recent years and we have been the poorer for it. For the eschatology of Easter must be a constant component in our understanding of the event. Instead of being the end of the line, Easter is really just the beginning, a beginning which will find its culmination only in that everlasting kingdom which John is seeking to describe in his visions. As the author of the Letter to the Hebrews put it, we do not yet see that kingdom. But we do see Jesus, risen from the dead, crowned with glory and honor. And he whom we can see is the guarantee of that kingdom which we cannot see. But it is in the light of that unseen kingdom yet to come that we find the strength and the courage to witness in these kingdoms in which we dwell. Without the vision of Revelation, there could be no acts of the apostles—then or now.

The Fifth Sunday of Easter

Lutheran	Roman Catholic	Episcopal	Presbyterian and UCC
Acts 13:44–52	Acts 14:20b–26	Acts 13:44–52	Acts 14:19–28
Rev. 21:1–5	Rev. 21:1–5a	Rev. 19:1, 4–9	Rev. 21:1–5
John 13:31–35	John 13:31–35	John 13:31–35	John 13:31–35

EXEGESIS

First Lesson: Acts 13:44–52. The book of the Acts of the Apostles shows us the spread of the Christian movement from Jerusalem through Judea and Samaria "to the end of the earth" (1:8). In our section we observe a specific change in missionary strategy. For although from chap. 13 on Paul and Barnabas are sent out beyond the borders of Palestine, it had been their method to visit synagogues wherever they went and thus to reach Gentiles via the synagogues. The mission thus had been indirectly directed to Gentiles, especially to those who as God fearers attended the synagogue without becoming full-fledged proselytes. Now, however, Paul and Barnabas declare that they will turn to the Gentiles directly. They tell the Jews: "It was necessary that the word of God should be spoken first to you. Since you thrust it from you, and judge yourselves unworthy of eternal life, behold, we turn to the Gentiles" (v. 46). This missionary strategy is based on the prophecy of Isaiah 49: "I have set you to be a light for the Gentiles, that you may bring salvation to the uttermost parts of the earth" (v. 47). The apostles Paul and Barnabas understand themselves in the light of God's original purpose for Israel, because she or her remnant is addressed in Isaiah 49 as the "Servant of the Lord," whose task it is to be a light to the Gentiles. Thus missionary method is here combined with theological insight.

What caused this change in missionary strategy? It was due to the jealousy and stubbornness of the leaders of the synagogue. For although Paul had considerable success with his sermon in Antioch, as recorded in Acts 13:16–41, so that "the people begged that these things might be told them the next sabbath" (v. 42), and "the next sabbath almost the whole city gathered to hear the word of God" (v. 44), the jealousy of the Jews led to strife and persecution.

In the eyes of the author of Acts the Jews invoke God's judgment upon

The Fifth Sunday of Easter

themselves, whereas the Gentiles joyfully hear the gospel. Paul and Barnabas engage in a gesture of judgment toward the Jews by shaking "off the dust from their feet against them" (v. 51) and move on to Iconium.

Second Lesson: Rev. 21:1–5. At this point in the Revelation of John we have truly reached the end. After the terrible series of judgments in the foregoing chapters, espcially in chaps. 19 and 20, a new vision appears. It is the descent of the kingdom of God from heaven, here portrayed as a new heaven and a new earth with the new Jerusalem.

The new heaven and earth are dualistically set over against our present heaven and earth, which were the scene of terror, war, oppression, and martyrdom. Indeed the visionary states that "the first heaven and the first earth had passed away and the sea," the old symbol of darkness and chaos, "was no more." The new Jerusalem is "the Bride, the wife of the Lamb" (v. 9); it is the place of ultimate bliss for those who have been faithful in the present era of the first heaven and earth. It is here that God himself dwells with his people and "he will wipe away every tear from their eyes . . . for the former things have passed away" (v. 4).

What Paul had written about those who find themselves in Christ, about the new creation for which "the old has passed away, and the new has come" (2 Cor. 5:17), the author of the Revelation projects into the coming of the kingdom itself. Here we witness the essence of Christian hope, not only the hope that our individual lives will not end at death or that only individuals at death will be saved, but the hope that our whole creation will be radically transformed so that it will ultimately be the scene of God's presence.

Without God's ultimate victory over evil, death, and oppression, creation ceases to be God's domain and becomes a meaningless tragedy. And so the meaning of the resurrection becomes fully visible here. "Death shall be no more, neither shall there be mourning nor crying nor pain any more, for the former things have passed away" (v. 4). The resurrection proclaims Christ's victory over death and this undergirds the Christian hope in the ultimate victory of God. So the resurrection becomes the first sign of that victory, for it is here that death—the last enemy—has been decisively defeated.

Gospel: John 13:31–35. With John 13 we move to the second part of the Gospel. John 1–12 is often called the Book of Signs and John 13–20 (21) the Book of the Passion. It is well known that John's Gospel does not contain a eucharistic Last Supper. Instead there is a supper prior to the Farewell Discourses of chaps. 13–17 and the passion, which is celebrated in the liturgy of the church as Maundy Thursday. Jesus gives his disciples a new mandate at the supper on the day before the passion: "A new commandment I give to you, that you love one another" (v. 34). Prior to the commandment Jesus himself has acted it out by washing the feet of the disciples.

Our section starts out with the betrayal of Judas, which forebodes the beginning of the passion. Thus the author states solemnly: "So, after receiving the morsel, he immediately went out; and it was night" (v. 30). What follows comes as a surprise: no words about the tragedy of the night with its impending dark happenings, but words about glorification: "Now is the Son of man glorified and in him God is glorified" (v. 31). It belongs to the perspective of the Gospel of John that the crucifixion is seen so strongly in the light of the resurrection, and that the crucifixion itself is regarded as a glorification. Thus in John's Gospel the verb "to lift up" is used of the cross in two ways—as a lifting up of Jesus on the cross, but also as Jesus being lifted up into God's heavenly glory.

Thus the new commandment to love one another is given in the light of the glorification of the cross, of Jesus giving himself in love. It is therefore only new in this light, for in itself the new commandment is not new at all, but the OT commandment of Lev. 19:18.

There is a puzzling word on Jesus in this section which is characteristic of the Gospel of John. In v. 33 Jesus says: "Where I am going you cannot come." Peter takes Jesus up on this word in vv. 36 f. and asks him outright: "Lord, where are you going? . . . Why cannot I follow you now?" Jesus answers: not now, but later. This means that Jesus is being taken up to eternal life with the Father and that only later, after the gift of the Spirit, can the disciples follow him there.

HOMILETICAL INTERPRETATION

It is difficult for us to conceive what a traumatic experience it must have been for the early Christians to break all of the ties with their Jewish origins. More than anyone else, it was Paul who saw clearly that the break had to come, not simply because of the opposition which the church encountered from the synagogue, but even more because of the universalism which was implicit in the Christian gospel. It simply was not possible to confine the good news to an ethnic group or to a particular culture. Its dynamism had to reach out to involve the whole world.

Of course, nothing would have pleased Paul and his associates more than to have Israel as a part of this gospel outreach. If the old Israel of God could have moved on to become the new Israel, that would have been wonderful. It was that hope that made it "necessary that the word of God should be spoken first to you" (v. 46). But when that hope was frustrated, as it was in the passage recorded in the lesson from Acts, Paul did not go home to brood about it. He took it as a clear sign that the time had come to move out with the gospel into a larger world.

All that is history, but quite possibly a continuing history. It is no news that the churches of the Western world, both in Europe and America, are either stagnant or declining. What is news to many Western Christians is the fact that in parts of Africa and Asia the rate of Christian growth is no less than astounding. Much of this growth is ragged and out of control. It certainly does not follow the lines and patterns with which Western Christians are comfortable. But the fact remains that at this rate in just a few generations Nairobi or Djakarta may be more important as Christian capitals than Rome or Geneva. It is not impossible to suppose that by the year 2000 the Christian faith may be more relevant and vital in the Third World than it is in Europe or North America.

All that is speculative, but it gives some indication of the way in which this dynamic gospel still has a way of breaking free from the limits which we so carefully set for it. It is easy for us in many American cities to look down our churchly noses at the Hispanic Pentecostal or the black Baptist and be extremely critical of the way in which he does things. But the fact remains that things are getting done while many of our more traditional churches are still seeking to minister to congregations that are no longer there.

Paul's stubborn insistence that it was time to go to the Gentiles was not based on any Pauline anti-Semitism, but on the passionate conviction that the good news of the gospel was for the world. It was therefore useless to waste time arguing about it with people who basically were not interested. Even in Antioch the reception which the gospel received outside the synagogue circle was a strong indication that the time had come to move out and "bring salvation to the uttermost parts of the earth" (v. 47).

At the heart of many of the decisions which Paul and his friends had to make in these days was the *new commandment* which our Lord gave his disciples on the night of his betrayal: "Love one another; even as I have loved you." So long as it was possible to interpret that commandment in terms of their own small circle, the difficulties that the disciples had with it were minimal. But once the "one another" began to be enlarged to include all kinds of people, including many kinds that the disciples had been brought up to avoid, there were some real decisions to be made.

How far did Jesus intend to go with his "one another"? Who is to be included in the category "my disciples"? Thinking through his whole mission and message, they could come to only one conclusion. No limits could be set. Love for one another had to include Greek and barbarian, slave and free, Roman and African, as well as their own kind.

After all, to his command to love one another, Jesus had added a pretty strong qualifier: "even as I have loved you." They knew only too well what that meant, for the love of Jesus had never been selective, never been dependent on the qualities of the one to be loved—after all, he had loved even them! And they also knew how he had loved them to the end, stopping at nothing, not even his cross. How could they take the love of someone like that and claim that it was meant only for this group or for that class?

How can we?

One possible excuse could be the cost, as Paul and his friends discovered in Antioch. It is romantic foolishness to suppose that all the world loves Christian lovers; generally the world finds them horribly disturbing. But what is more disturbing is that Jesus, when he spoke these words, certainly knew what his love was about to cost him—yet he spoke of that cost in terms of "glory." Perhaps our problem is that we find humiliation and pain difficult to reconcile with our idea of glory.

In America we Christians have never quite rid ourselves of the notion that glory has to mean success, and we have cut our course accordingly. In our country, the glorious church is the successful church, lots of people, big budgets, extravagant buildings. For Jesus (and for Paul) the only real glory was the cost of love. God was glorified in Jesus when his obedient love accepted the cross. Christ is glorified in his people when they accept the price of that same obedient love, whatever may be the circumstance.

The Fifth Sunday of Easter

It is unfortunate that for many of us Christians the great NT word *love* has lost its meaning and been reduced to a harmless feeling of goodwill. We need continually to remind ourselves that in the gospel love is always cross-shaped, whether it be Christ's love for God, for us, or our love for the brethren. If we would remember that, we might find ourselves using the word far less carelessly and cheaply than we often do.

Over against all of our attempts to universalize the love of Christ in our own lives and actions the lesson from Revelation reminds us of that completed community of perfect love, the holy city that comes down from God out of heaven. It will never come here, not even in response to our keenest efforts, yet in a real sense it is already here for even now we are citizens of it.

This perfect community against which all our communities are judged has two main characteristics. On the positive side, it is directly and openly the habitation of God. To be sure, the NT says that about the Christian community even now: "You are the temple of God." But even as we believe that, we have to admit how many temporal and personal factors conspire to prevent anything like its full realization. Our own self-interests, our own spirits, to say nothing of the spirit of the age in which we live—all these make God's presence in the midst of his people partial and interrupted. In the holy city all such things have disappeared —"the dwelling of God is with men."

On the negative side, the fulfilled community will no longer be prevented from loving by the risks and the costs which so often get in our way here. No more tears, no more death, no more mourning or crying, no more pain—"the former things have passed away." For those who have used these as a rationalization for the refusal to love, there will be no excuses. For those who have regretted the way in which these things have limited their loving, there will be no more limitations.

The wonderful promise which undergirds both what is and what is to be is that word in v. 5: "Behold, I am making all things new." This is true and trustworthy, and because he is making all things new—even our stubborn refusals and our selfish satisfactions—the holy city can even now be dimly glimpsed, even in the midst of our cities of failure and despair.

The Sixth Sunday of Easter

Lutheran	*Roman Catholic*	*Episcopal*	*Presbyterian and UCC*
Acts 15:1–2, 22–29	Acts 15:1–2, 22–29	Acts 15:1–6, 22–29	Acts 15:1–2, 22–29
Rev. 21:10–14, 22–23	Rev. 21:10–14, 21–23	Rev. 21:2–4, 14, 22–24	Rev. 21:10–14, 22–23
John 14:23–29	John 14:23–29	John 14:23–29	John 14:23–29

EXEGESIS

First Lesson: Acts 15:1-2, 22-29. Acts 15 brings us to a critical juncture in the Book of Acts. It reports the first apostolic council of the church, which was held in Jerusalem. It is a critical juncture because the future of the mission to the Gentiles is at stake, and with it, therefore, the future of the church as such.

What was happening? Paul and Barnabas had been sent out by the church of Antioch on missionary activity and in the course of their mission had preached the gospel to Gentiles, having made it a point to turn exclusively to the Gentiles after the Jews had rejected their message (13:46, 47). Upon returning to Antioch they gave a report of their mission and "declared all that God had done with them, and how he had opened a door of faith to the Gentiles" (14:27). Trouble ensued when people came down from Jerusalem and insisted that Gentiles could not become members of the church unless they were circumcised, that is, unless they first became Jews. When Paul and Barnabas protested this, they and others were sent to Jerusalem to put the problem before the apostles and elders.

The critical question was this: Is the Christian promise of salvation only valid for the Jews, the sons of Abraham, and is it, therefore, necessary for everyone who desires to become a Christian to become a Jew first? Or is the Christian promise of salvation a universal one, which includes the Gentiles on an equal basis with the Jews? The question circles essentially around the function of the Mosaic law within a Christian framework. Paul struggled with this question throughout his missionary career and refused to give the law an essential place in the preaching of the gospel.

A historic decision is reached by the council in Jerusalem. After listening to Peter, Barnabas, and Paul, James as president of the council issues a statement in which, basically, the Gentile mission without circumcision is approved. A letter to this effect is sent to the churches in Antioch, Syria, and Cilicia, in which the guidance of the Holy Spirit is highlighted: "It has seemed good to the Holy Spirit and to us to lay upon you no greater burden than these necessary things" (v. 28). What follows is the so-called Apostolic Decree which merely lists some Noachian commandments, certain moral precepts which every Gentile must keep.

Second Lesson: Rev. 21:10–14, 22–23. This passage gives us a vision of the new Jerusalem as the coming kingdom of God. Yet it is as well a vision of the church triumphant. It is the ecumenical church which is described here in its perfection, for in that way we must understand the repetitious use of the number twelve. The twelve gates of the city have as guardians twelve angels; on the gates are written the names of the twelve tribes of Israel and the twelve foundations of the wall carry the names of the twelve apostles (vv. 12–14) and are adorned with twelve jewels (vv. 19–20).

Because the new Jerusalem is the wife of the Lamb (v. 9) and the kingdom of God it has no need of a temple anymore, "for its temple is the Lord God the Almighty and the Lamb" (v. 22). And because of the presence of God in it, it is a perfect city where all earthly conditions are made unnecessary (vv. 23–25). Those who belong to this evil world are banned: it is a city for the faithful only, those whose names are written in the "Lamb's book of life" (v. 27). The vision then is one of joy, but also one of judgment: "nothing unclean shall enter it" (v. 27). Yet by its light the nations shall walk.

We waver in describing the new Jerusalem because in the vision of the new Jerusalem the vision of the kingdom of God and the triumphant church seem to merge and coalesce. There is no need in the city for a temple (v. 22) because in one sense all of the city is a temple directed to the worship of the presence of God. There is no need for a church, yet the foundations of the city carry the twelve names of the twelve apostles of the Lamb.

The vision of the holy city, Jerusalem, coming down out of heaven from God raises the question of the relation between the church and the kingdom of God. The new Jerusalem with the names of the twelve apostles is a picture of the triumphant church. Yet there is no temple in the city! Thus in the living presence of God himself the triumphant church and the kingdom of God merge into one. For in one sense kingdom of God and triumphant church form a unity, once the church triumphant includes all creation in it and once this new Jerusalem becomes the light for all the nations (v. 24).

Gospel: John 14:23-29. With John 14 we are in the midst of the Farewell Discourses. It seems as if these Farewell Discourses are post-resurrection speeches, because the victory of the resurrection shines through them. Jesus speaks about the unity of himself with the Father and about their unity with the disciples (vv. 23 and 24). These speeches are really monologues; the questions of the disciples function only to keep the monologue going and to introduce essential points about Jesus' relation to the Father and his imminent going away to the Father via cross and resurrection. Although Jesus is still with the disciples before the events of passion and resurrection, he speaks as if these future events have already taken place.

In our section he announces the gift of the Holy Spirit. The Holy Spirit is called the "Paraclete" in the Gospel of John, which means an advocate for the defense. The Paraclete is the one who comforts and counsels. Therefore the RSV translates the word as "Counselor" (v. 25). What is the function of the Holy Spirit? He is, as it were, Jesus' substitute; he is "the other Counselor" (v. 15), who after Jesus' departure will be with the disciples, who will "teach you all things and bring to your remembrance all that I have said to you." At times it seems as if the Spirit is not so much the substitute for Jesus until he returns at the parousia but rather Jesus himself in a different mode of presence—the Jesus who after the resurrection will be seen by his disciples. "I will not leave you desolate; I will come to you. Yet a little while and the world will see me no more, but you will see me; because I live, you will live also" (vv. 18, 19).

The Jesus who is going to the cross is likewise going to the Father. Therefore he can give the disciples his peace, the peace of victory over an evil world (v. 27). He exhorts the disciples to rejoice, "because I go to the Father" (v. 28). The remarkable thing in the Gospel of John is the telescoping of cross and resurrection. Thus Jesus' going away to the cross is likewise both his going away to the Father and the promised coming of the Holy Spirit. Everything here seems predetermined. Jesus

The Sixth Sunday of Easter

predicts the coming of the ruler of this world (v. 30), for it is he who is responsible for the crucifixion. Yet the ruler of this world has no power over Jesus (v. 30), since he is merely doing his predetermined task.

HOMILETICAL INTERPRETATION

"It seemed good to the Holy Spirit and to us." Those words with which the apostles end their meeting in Jerusalem may strike us as presumptuous, but they really summarize the basic premise by which the people of God function in this world.

The exact details of the dispute which caused this Jerusalem meeting need not detain us here. They are closely related to the whole matter of the dependence of the Christian gospel upon its Jewish inheritance. The exegesis fills in what some of the specific questions were. Our point is simply that they had caused a division which seriously threatened the unity of the early church.

Nor is it necessary for us to become involved with the exact details of the settlement. To be truthful, scholars have never agreed exactly what they were or exactly how they are to be interpreted. Once again our point is a simple one. The rift was closed and the settlement of the dispute was laid to the Holy Spirit working through Christian people. "It seemed good to the Holy Spirit and to us."

Now it would be difficult to imagine two men who, in spite of their deep commitment to Jesus Christ, came at the Christian gospel from more different directions than the two principals in this dispute. Paul was passionately devoted to sharing the good news with the Gentile world; James was equally concerned with the preservation of sound biblical (OT) tradition in the infant church. While nobody could really question the correctness of either man's motives, under ordinary circumstances their positions would have been strong enough to split the church. But the church remained together with both Paul and James as leaders, unwilling to lay any unnecessary burdens on the people of God other than a basic moral stance and a common loyalty to Jesus Christ.

In the time in which we are living we hear a great deal about the Spirit as a private gift, but we hear little about the gift of the Spirit to the church, which is at least as important, if not a more important emphasis in the NT. It is, of course, easy for us to identify our ecclesiastical decisions with the voice of the Spirit—and that has happened all too often in Christian history. But it is equally easy to grow cynical about the Lord's guidance of his people through his Spirit without which the story of the church in history is pretty meaningless.

Though it could be dangerous to generalize, it would seem to be pretty clear from the story in Acts that the unity of Christ's people comes from the leading of the Spirit and that divisiveness and fracturing are the work of human pride and prejudice. There is an old saying, attributed to an early father of the church, which reads, "In all essentials, unity; in all nonessentials, liberty; in everything, charity." Without quibbling about what are essentials and what are nonessentials, it is possible to say that that father understood the leading of the Spirit.

Most of what our Lord had to say in today's Gospel lesson is also concerned with the Spirit. There is a lot of loose talk among some Christians about the "second coming," referring to Christ's coming again in glory at the end of time. John is not unfamiliar with such an idea, but for him the real second coming is the coming in the Spirit—both Father and Son are with their own through the presence of the Spirit.

Indeed it is the Spirit who makes Christ and his will real to the disciple. We are not left merely with a history book or a commentary, helpful as these may be. We have a living presence which is continually interpreting to us what the will of Christ is in any given situation, as happened in the case of the assembly at Jerusalem. This is why in the passage before us Jesus could use such a paradoxical statement as "I go away, and I will come to you" (v. 28). His going away to the Father through the events of Good Friday and Easter was simply the prelude to his return and continued abiding through the Spirit.

But it must also be pointed out that this coming of Christ through the Spirit has an important precondition. The coming is to the man "who loves me and keeps my words." The will to obedience, which is our Lord's own description of what it means to love him, is the door through which the Spirit makes his entrance. The mere crooning of "My Jesus, I Love Thee" will not do; there must be a style of life which is serious about servanthood.

While it is not up to us to judge the charismatics who have recently taken the center of today's Christian stage, one could wish that many of them understood that the Spirit is not given to just anyone. Glossolalia combined with racial hatred, for example, makes the claim to the Spirit very suspect indeed. So far as John's understanding is concerned, there

The Sixth Sunday of Easter

is a direct connection between Spirit and servanthood, since servanthood is the precise example which our Lord gave his disciples.

John also sees a connection between the Spirit and peace. In the midst of a situation that is fraught with danger, a situation that will make hearts troubled and afraid, Jesus offers peace to his disciples, a peace that can in no way be affected by the world around them (v. 27). But that peace would be little more than a cruel joke were it not for the promise of the Spirit who will bring both certainty and security to those who are serious about the purposes which he will help them understand.

The word which Jesus uses for the Spirit, "the Paraclete," is one for which there is no good English equivalent. Comforter, Counselor, Teacher, Advocate, Helper—these are some of the translations used in different versions. In situations where the office exists, "ombudsman" might not be a bad translation. The wide variety of translations is necessary because all of them are involved in Jesus' understanding of the work of the Spirit when he described him as "the Paraclete." But all of them are words which indicate a function which assists us to become responsible and committed servants of Jesus and his kingdom.

The continuation of John's vision of the holy city in the lesson from his revelation mentions the Spirit only once when it says that it was in the Spirit that he was carried away to a high mountain to see the new Jerusalem (v. 10). But even though the Spirit is not mentioned, it is the Spirit that is really at the center of that vision. For in the holy city there is no temple (v. 22). No temple is necessary because the vision and perception of God and Christ are immediate.

But that is precisely the function of the Spirit here. Though the vision is incomplete and the perceptions are always partial, the Spirit seeks to make the Father and the Son directly real to us. Books and churches, sacraments and sermons are only some of the means which he employs to confront us directly with the presence of God in Christ. At the end, in the holy city, means will no longer be necessary, but the Spirit will still be doing the same task.

There can be no doubt that many of the extravagances of present day Pentecostalism are part of the penalty which we in the traditional churches must pay for our long neglect of the Spirit. Was it not Cardinal Newman who once said that "every heresy is the revenge of a forgotten truth"? So there is doubtless much that we need to learn from the charismatic movement. But we must never learn it at the expense of the other lesson which the church has learned so bitterly in the past few years—that we are the servant people of a servant Lord. In the NT, servanthood and the Spirit belong closely together and together they make for a style of discipleship that is faithful and convincing.

The Ascension of Our Lord

Lutheran	*Roman Catholic*	*Episcopal*	*Presbyterian and UCC*
Acts 1:1–11	Acts 1:1–11	Acts 1:1–11	Acts 1:1–11
Eph. 1:16–23	Eph. 1:17–23	Eph. 1:16–23	Eph. 1:16–23
Luke 24:44–53	Luke 24:46–53	Luke 24:49–53	Luke 24:44–53

EXEGESIS

First Lesson: Acts 1:1-11. The first chapter of the Book of Acts is crucial for understanding the rest of the book. It not only recapitulates what the author has written in his first book, the Gospel of Luke, and thus connects the two books, but it also sets the theme for the present book. Whereas the final verses of the Gospel leave us uncertain whether Luke reports Jesus' ascension to us, the author here makes it clear that Jesus appeared to his disciples for forty days, instructing them about the kingdom of God, before he was taken away from them in the ascension. At the same time Jesus commands the disciples not to leave Jerusalem, but to await in Jerusalem the gift of the Spirit, Pentecost.

Resurrection means end time, the dawning of the kingdom of God and its first beginning. It is therefore natural that the disciples ask Jesus: "Lord, will you at this time restore the kingdom to Israel?" (v. 6). What now follows is crucial for the theology of the author: he wants to prevent the Christian movement from turning into a narrow sectarian Jewish group which concentrates on the coming kingdom of God, passively awaiting its descent from heaven. The charge of the hour is not a passive waiting, but mission. Therefore the moment of the ascension is the door to the gift of the Spirit, whereas the gift of the Spirit is the power behind the mission of the church.

The Ascension of Our Lord

It is not now the time for the arrival of the kingdom of God, but men must prepare the world for it through mission. Twice in our section a passive waiting for the supernatural advent of the kingdom is rejected. First, when the disciples want to know when the kingdom will come (v. 6); second, when the two men in white robes at the ascension urge the disciples not to keep staring into heaven, expecting the kingdom to come, but to be at their business, which is to be Jesus' witnesses "in Jerusalem and in all Judea and Samaria and to the end of the earth" (v. 8).

Sometimes the Acts of the Apostles is called the Acts of the Holy Spirit. The theme of this opening chapter of Acts makes it clear that no witnessing is possible without the Holy Spirit: "But you shall receive power when the Holy Spirit has come upon you" (v. 8). The kingdom of God and its coming are not denied in the opening chapter, but the way to them must be prepared by the missionary drive of the church under the guidance of the Spirit.

Second Lesson: Eph. 1:16–23. Until the present time scholarship has had two difficulties with Paul's letter to the Ephesians. In the first place, Pauline authorship has been questioned and in the second place it has been doubted whether the letter was directed to Ephesus at all. Some of the reasons for these doubts are the omission of "at Ephesus" at the opening of the letter in the better manuscripts and the absence of any greetings to members of the church in the final chapter. Pauline authorship has been questioned mainly because of the peculiar liturgical style and the awkward syntax of the letter.

However, since the basic ideas of the letter are Pauline, it does not matter so much whether we ascribe the letter to Paul himself or to one of his pupils. Whether the address is to Ephesus or not does not detract from the importance of the letter.

In our section Paul gives thanks for the faith and love of the church and intercedes for its members in his prayers. What he wishes for them is "having the eyes of your hearts enlightened, that you may know what is the hope to which he has called you" (v. 18). What then is the basis for this hope? It is the resurrection of Christ because the resurrection means the exaltation and enthronement of Christ at the right hand of the Father. Thus it means the victory over all the hostile powers of this world which seem to mock the Christian hope. The resurrection thus has cosmic significance: it is not just the resuscitation of a dead man, but it signifies the victory over all those forces in the world which imprison and frighten Christians. Once we are anchored in Christ and his victory, once we belong to the church as the body of Christ, we are lifted above all the obstacles which seem to deny our salvation. For God "has put all things under his feet and has made him the head over all things for the church, which is his body, the fullness of him who fills all in all" (vv. 22 f.). Since his resurrection Christ reigns over all the spiritual forces in this world, which now must pay homage to him. The church as the body of Christ is the guarantee in this world of Christ's cosmic reign over all things and the growth of the church will finally embrace the whole creation.

Gospel: Luke 24:44-53. For a general discussion and outline of Luke 24 see the exegetical treatment of the Gospels for Easter Day and Easter Evening, above, pp. 3-4 and pp. 10-11.

Luke 24:44-53 occurs in the midst of the third section of this chapter, where Christ appears to the disciples in the upper room and demonstrates to them the continuing identity between the Jesus they have known and his present appearance as the Christ. This continuing identity is especially stressed in the words with which Christ addresses them (vv. 38 f.). Jesus here opens the minds of the disciples so that they understand the Scriptures. Luke has Jesus expound here the history of God with Israel as a history of salvation climaxing in his death and resurrection and in the purpose of his death and resurrection, which is the establishment of the universal mission of the church to mankind to offer them repentance and forgiveness of sins. Thus the risen Christ appoints the disciples to their missionary task.

But before this task can begin they must wait in Jerusalem for the day of Pentecost which will give them the power of the Spirit for their task. Thus after Jesus' parting from them the disciples return to the temple in Jerusalem in expectation of the promise of the Spirit. Our section stresses that God's salvation history of Israel climaxes in Jesus' death and resurrection and that the apostolic church will continue God's salvation history, when it has been constituted as the new Israel which fulfills God's plan. The apostolic church thus is the new Israel which preaches the power of the resurrection to the world and which translates the meaning of the resurrection as repentance and forgiveness for all nations.

HOMILETICAL INTERPRETATION

Surely everyone can remember the flap created some years ago by the appearance of Bishop Robinson's book *Honest to God* and its scathing attack on the three-storied universe which the bishop claimed is implied in the ascension narrative and which he asserted is something no twentieth century man can be expected to accept. After such a withering attack, one might well tremble before an Ascension Day sermon.

But the bishop wrote that a decade or so ago and in the intervening years, hopefully, we have learned something. We have learned, for example, that *up* still says something symbolically even in a universe in which it is literally impossible to determine which way *up* is. But more importantly, theologians have recently begun to learn again that there are some truths which can never be communicated by concepts nearly so well as they can be conveyed by a narrative. What we need to do is not to try to *demythologize* the story but listen to what it has to say. Christmas and Easter are outstanding examples of stories that need to be listened to rather than demythologized, but so is the ascension.

Perhaps I can add a word of personal testimony. When I was in my first year in the ministry and learned that my parish held an Ascension Day service, I wanted to be ill that Thursday because the ascension was something I had never thought about in seminary except to dismiss it as a hopeless myth. But after twenty-eight Ascension Days, I have found it one of my favorite festivals which I shall greatly miss now that I am no longer a parish minister.

The narrative itself is told twice by Luke, once at the end of his Gospel and once at the beginning of Acts. There is one emphasis in both versions which is worth noting and that is the emphasis on the word "witness." In the Gospel account, the word is simply mentioned as the disciples' responsibility in view of the summary of his gospel which Jesus has given them (vv. 45–48).

In the account in Acts, the dialogue is given in somewhat more detail. Incredibly enough (but not so incredibly if you know disciples like us), the apostles are still hung up on their idea of a restored Israel and want to know if now is the time for the restoration (v. 6). Jesus gently reminds them that the setting of times and predicting of seasons is not their business; their job is to witness in ever widening circles until the whole world knows (vv. 8–9). The account closes with the two attendant figures reminding the disciples to stop looking up into heaven and with notice of the disciples' return to Jerusalem.

Both narratives have a great deal to say; but it is the passage from Paul's letter to the Ephesians (today's Second Lesson) which interprets the meaning of the story in particularly significant concepts. Paul's ideas about the ascension appear in a series of phrases, each one of which is so packed with meaning that it could provide more than one sermon for the ascension festival. Let us try to analyze them briefly.

1. "At the right hand" (v. 20): Obviously, God has no right hand—a fact which Paul knew as well as any of us! But we may need to be reminded that in an imperial court, from which Paul was drawing his metaphor, the right hand is the place of power, the place occupied by the vice-regent who is charged with the execution of the royal purpose.

If Jesus Christ is the executor of God's purposes, then he must be the accurate representative of those purposes. God's purposes for his world can be summarized in Jesus Christ, and the ascension is the final declaration that this is so. If anyone asks where the world is going, now the answer is plain. Jesus Christ is the answer. The ascension to the right hand is the Father's forthright declaration of his purposes for his world.

A word must be said to remind us that he who sits at the right hand is he who was raised from the dead, that is, he who took upon him the form of a servant and was obedient unto death. So far as human history and destiny are concerned, their Lord is no stranger but one who has fully shared them. To use Karl Barth's phrase, the ascension is the permanent guarantee of the *humanity of God*.

2. "Far above all rule and authority and power and dominion": In a day in which we are all programmed to think that our destiny depends on the great men of the time, the men in the White House or the Kremlin or wherever, the ascension reminds us of the real limits of their power, invisible as those limits may seem in the press or on TV.

The ascension is a healthy corrective for Christians who easily get mixed up as to who is in charge. King Jesus on his throne has survived all kinds of kings, emperors, princes, captains of industry, barons of finance, etc., who assumed that the world belonged to them. It is important to know who is in charge when we must decide whom we shall serve.

Many Christian critics of our society have observed the phenomenon of *civil religion*, the confusion of the American way of life with the

The Ascension of Our Lord

kingdom of God. I am not arguing that the neglect of a festival can distort a man's faith, but I am claiming that such a confusion is impossible for anyone who takes the ascension seriously. There is only one final authority and one final loyalty—far above all other rule and authority.

There can be no doubt that when Paul used this pile-up of phrases he had far more in mind than temporal or economic power. He was thinking also of those "spirits in the air," which in his day were commonly believed to influence the human story, and he was asserting that Jesus was also in control of them. We may or may not share Paul's belief in such beings, but we must share his conviction that all the impersonal systems and structures which exercise enormous control over human affairs are not final and absolute but are in the power of King Jesus.

3. "In this age but also in that which is to come": Not only the present, but the future is in the control of the ascended Lord. Paul is talking not just of the future of the church, but of the future of the world! Naturally, it is impossible for us to guess the directions in which that control will move or the reasons for those directions. But that the future belongs to Jesus Christ and not to any one of the half-dozen claimants squabbling over it at any given time—that's the ascension faith.

If the Marxists have made converts in the Christian world because they offer a philosophy of history, again it is because the Christian church has muffled its own ascension gospel which is as complete a philosophy of history as can be found. I like the typical symbol found in the dome of the apse of many Orthodox churches. It depicts King Jesus sitting on his throne and in his right hand are a globe and a cross. It simply says in one way what the old spiritual says in another, "He's got the whole world in his hands."

4. "The immeasurable greatness of his power in us who believe" (v. 19): To be sure, this phrase appears before the others which we have been considering, but now perhaps "the immeasurable greatness" begins to have some specifications. It is as the servants of this mighty conqueror that we confront the world. It is as the brothers of this sovereign that we do our witnessing in our communities. It is as those who already share all that their Lord has that we take up our crosses.

Certainly there is much in the picture of Jesus the teacher from Nazareth. Certainly there is much in the traditional version of Jesus the Good Shepherd. And we can never turn our backs on the figure of Jesus on his cross. But our Christianity has been unnecessarily crippled because it has so largely lost the vision of Jesus the cosmic and universal sovereign with all power in his hands. Whatever may be the difficulties of modern man with the cosmology of the ascension narrative, the difficulties of a gospel which omits the Christ who conquers now and is still to conquer are even greater.

The Seventh Sunday of Easter

Lutheran	Roman Catholic	Episcopal	Presbyterian and UCC
Acts 7:55–60	Acts 7:55–60	Acts 7:55–60	Acts 7:55–60
Rev. 22:12–14, 16–17, 20	Rev. 22:12–14, 16–17, 20	Rev. 22:12–14, 16–17, 20	Rev. 22:12–14, 16–17, 20
John 17:20–26	John 17:20–26	John 17:20–26	John 17:20–26

EXEGESIS

First Lesson: Acts 7:55-60. This episode might well be entitled, "The Blood of the Martyrs Is the Seed of the Church," for it reports the first martyrdom of the early church, that of Stephen, one of the seven deacons appointed by the apostles to serve tables as told in Acts 6. The "seven" may have been deacons, but more important than that, they were also evangelists. And it is as evangelists that we meet them: Stephen here in Acts 6 and 7; Philip in Acts 8 and Acts 21:8, where he is called "the evangelist."

The story of Stephen's martyrdom comes after he has given a long sermon, recounting God's history of salvation with Israel, the promise of a redeemer in Jesus, and climaxing in a prophetic denunciation of the Jews: "You stiff-necked people, uncircumcised in heart and ears, you always resist the Holy Spirit. As your fathers did, so do you. Which of the prophets did not your fathers persecute? And they killed those who announced beforehand the coming of the Righteous One, whom you have now betrayed and murdered" (vv. 51-52).

Stephen's martyrdom reminds us that the story of the resurrection of

Jesus is not always a success story. Resurrection implies a missionary witness, as Luke 24 especially makes clear. But this missionary witness must carry a historical burden, the burden of resistance and persecution. Yet in the story of Acts the blood of the martyrs is the seed of the church. This is the first example of this theme in Acts. For, according to Acts, Saul is present as a witness to the martyrdom of Stephen. And as Acts 8:1 has it, he "was consenting to his death." Yet Saul was to become Paul shortly thereafter, the greatest apostolic witness of the early church. One cannot but wonder whether his presence at Stephen's death was not one of the factors which led to Paul's conversion as reported in Acts 9, when he is suddenly struck by Christ on the Damascus road.

We notice in Stephen's martyrdom how the story of Jesus' execution influenced other martyrdom stories. For while Stephen sees the heavens opened and the Son of man standing at the right hand of God, we are reminded twice of Jesus' words on the cross when Stephen prays: "Lord Jesus receive my spirit" and "Lord, do not hold this sin against them" (vv. 59 and 60; cf. Luke 23:34, 46).

Second Lesson: Rev. 22:12–14, 16–17, 20. The last chapter of Revelation contains the end of the seer's visions, closing with that of the new heaven and new earth and the new Jerusalem. What remain are the closing words to the churches (v. 16). We witness here concretely the role of the NT prophet. He is so identified with the Spirit and Jesus Christ that Jesus Christ speaks through him in the first person. In other words, he has become a mouthpiece for Jesus Christ: "Behold, I am coming soon, bringing my recompense . . . I am the Alpha and the Omega" (vv. 12–13). Yet the prophet is only at specific times the voice of Jesus Christ. At other times he knows to distinguish himself. In v. 20 we see the reciprocal relation of Jesus Christ and the prophet: "Surely I am coming soon! Amen. Come, Lord Jesus!"

It becomes clear why eschatological impulse cannot be absent from any Christian scheme of things. The prayer for the coming of Jesus is answered by the promise: "Surely I am coming soon" (v. 20; cf. v. 12). Christian hope is characterized by hope for the coming presence of Christ, who will make all things new (21:5) and who will ban from the world the old present order of injustice, oppression, and death.

Christian hope is not satisfied with a heavenly promise for individuals; it has a universal cosmic scope, so that it involves all of creation. The prayer for the coming of Jesus means a prayer for the coming of a new heaven and a new earth, where the kingdom of God will find its visible manifestation.

He who was the first, the Alpha, shall also be the last, the Omega (v. 13). Christ is here portrayed as the creator and judge, who decides who will have "the right to the tree of life" (v. 14), who may enter the heavenly city, and who must remain outside.

Gospel: John 17:20–26. The high priestly prayer in John 17 is the climax to the Farewell Discourses in the upper room of chaps. 13–17, but in another way the prayer is also the high point of the Gospel as such. Here the purpose of the sending of the Son, the aim of the incarnation, is fully set forth. There is a vision here of Jesus' "own," "the men whom thou gavest me out of the world" (v. 6), those "who have kept thy word" (v. 6). But this vision of Jesus' "own" in our section, vv. 20–26, is not limited to a spiritualist elite. It opens up a vision of the true ecumenical church: "I do not pray for these only, but also for those who believe in me through their word" (v. 20).

The picture of the ecumenical church is constituted by several features: (1) It is the church which is defined by mission, by going out into the world to recruit (v. 20). (2) It is the church which is constituted by a perfect unity, a unity which is grounded in the unity of the Father and the Son (v. 21). (3) This unity must be manifest in the world, so that it may perform in its unity a missionary appeal, "so that the world may know that thou hast sent me and hast loved them even as thou hast loved me" (v. 23). (4) The unity of the church is basically a unity of love, that is, the reflection of the mutual love of Father and Son, but even more a demonstration of the Father's infinite love for his people in the world. In this context we should notice the phrase, so often repeated in the Gospel of John: "he who has sent me." It occurs twenty-one times in the Gospel and receives in John 17 its outspoken clarification: "so that the world may know that thou hast loved me" (v. 23). Thus the sending of the Son is motivated by the infinite compassion of the Father for his own in the world. (5) The ecumenical church has an eschatological dimension. It participates in the glory of the Father and the Son and looks forward to the time when it will be "with me where I am, to behold my glory which thou hast given me in thy love for me before the foundation of the world" (v. 24).

The Seventh Sunday of Easter

HOMILETICAL INTERPRETATION

Traditionally the church has celebrated St. Stephen's Day on the day after Christmas. T. S. Eliot, in his play *Murder in the Cathedral*, has Archbishop Becket preach an interesting sermon linking the birth of Jesus with the martyrdom of Stephen. But in terms of Christian logic, there would seem to be more point in placing Stephen directly after the ascension.

For certainly the vision which strengthened the first martyr in his last agony was neither that of the infant or the crucified Jesus, but the vision of the ascended and sovereign Lord. "I see the heavens opened, and the Son of man standing at the right hand of God" (v. 56). If what we tried to say about the meaning of the ascension had any validity whatever, then Stephen is its outstanding demonstration. It was precisely because he was certain about the ultimate lordship of Jesus that he could stand up to his persecutors.

But more than that. No one who reads the story of Stephen's death can fail to be impressed by the similarity of his last word, "Lord, do not hold this sin against them" (v. 60) with the first of Jesus' seven last words from the cross, "Father, forgive them for they know not what they do." That similarity is not the result of any artfulness on Luke's part. It is the result of Stephen's acceptance of obedience to Christ's word as part of the acceptance of his lordship. No man could and no man would make this kind of prayer in this kind of situation if he did not know whose he was and whom he served.

It is also good to be reminded that those who accept the sovereignty of the ascended Christ will not themselves move through the world in triumph. The church that says "Jesus is King" and is serious about that commitment is more likely to be stoned than successful. If servanthood be the form of obedience to which we are called, we need to remember that it is likely to be suffering servanthood. Stephen is a good indication of how it goes. But more important than that reminder is the fact that it is the vision of the one at the right hand of God that makes even our suffering victorious.

John's last vision in Revelation looks forward to that final hour when the ascended Lord will indeed have all things under him. The figure is an awesome one, Alpha and Omega, the beginning and the end, the standard by whom all men will be judged. But what is fascinating is the way in which in both v. 17 and the final verse of the vision the word "come" is used in a variety of ways.

"The Spirit and the Bride say, 'Come' "—but to whom are they saying it? Are they inviting the hearer to *come*, or are they beseeching the king to *come* and bring all things to an end? Or are they doing both? In the second half of the verse there can be no doubt. The invitation to *come* is opened wide to all. The ascended king has not lost his human heart. The one who invited all the weary and heavy-laden to *come* to him for refreshment still invites the thirsty to *come* to the water that gives life.

Now for a look at that final section of our Lord's great high priestly prayer which is today's Gospel. At the outset it should be said that no section of the Gospel has been subject to more misinterpretation in a good cause than these verses. The unity of Christ's people is certainly a constant theme in the NT and was obviously a concern of the blessed Lord himself. But the unity of Christ's people in the sense of the organic merger of denominations is obviously not what these words have in mind and to use them as a proof text for such proposals is to miss their point sadly.

It is, of course, possible that this kind of church union is a logical derivative of the unity for which our Lord prayed, but before we make that kind of assertion, we had best know something more about the unity which he mentioned in his prayer. That unity, in the first instance, must be the same kind of unity as the unity of the Father and the Son. There are many depths of meaning in such a phrase, but the most obvious one is a unity of purpose. The Father and the Son were one in their redemptive purpose so that the works of the Son were the intention of the Father. A similar unity of redemptive purpose is what must bind the church together. That it is such a redemptive purpose that Jesus has in mind is evidenced by the further word that he adds, "that the world may believe that thou hast sent me" (v. 21). A unity of the church with the purposes of the Father declared in the Son—such a concept far transcends (though it does not necessarily deny) a merger between two denominations.

Unhappily the unity on which the church has so often insisted in history has not been that kind of unity. It has been a unity in opinion, a unity in ritual, a unity in organization, the insistence upon which has led to schisms, persecutions, and even ecclesiastical murder! A unity in redemptive purpose is something which an individual congregation can

The Seventh Sunday of Easter

well examine. Even though all members have the same label and subscribe to the same creeds and confessions, there is no guarantee that they have achieved unity in the sense which this prayer envisions.

A further confirmation of Jesus' intention is to be found in John's peculiar use of the word "glory." "The glory which thou hast given me I have given to them, that they may be one even as we are one" (v. 22). John's use of "glory" is one on which whole studies have been made, but it can be said simply that it involves both the cross and the resurrection and not just the latter. The "glory" of Jesus is just as visible on Calvary on Good Friday as it was on Easter morning.

If that "glory" has been given to the disciples, it has to be the glory of sacrificial obedience—and that is the redemptive purpose of the Father worked out in terms of our own situations. If disciples are one in this, there can be all kinds of latitude in terms of theological opinion, all kinds of tolerance in terms of liturgical practice. But if the church is not at one in this, then no amount of theological or liturgical uniformity will ever be able to compensate for it.

The prayer ends by carrying the little church forward into the future: "Father, I desire that they also whom thou hast given me may be with me where I am, to behold my glory which thou hast given me in thy love for me before the foundation of the world" (v. 24). No doubt the obvious layer of meaning in this petition involves the little church's sharing in the final glory and triumph of the risen Lord, that they may see him as he is and enjoy him forever.

While that meaning cannot be denied, it is not usually the way in which John interprets Jesus' thinking. In John's understanding, more important than this ultimate reality is the ability to share in it now. Dr. A. E. Harvey puts it in this way (*Companion to the New Testament*, p. 376):

> The whole of the discourse has been exploring the manner in which Jesus would continue to be present with his disciples after the crucifixion and resurrection. Something of heaven, he has been saying, would attend their life on earth. But one could put it the other way round. It was not only that life in this world would be transformed by influences from another world: human beings, while still in this world, could have an experience of heaven. This was the climax of the possibilities of Christian discipleship, and the final subject of Jesus' great prayer for his followers.
>
> "The Spirit and the Bride say 'Come!'"
>
> Even so, *come*, Lord Jesus!